MAID MARIAN
MYTH or LEGEND?

MAID MARIAN
MYTH OR LEGEND?

Unveiling the Truth Behind Robin Hood's Lady Love,
the Heroine of Sherwood Forest

LYDIA–JANE PLANTE

MAID MARIAN — Myth or Legend?
Unveiling the Truth Behind Robin Hood's Lady Love,
the Heroine of Sherwood Forest

First published in 2025 by:

 *PRINCELY PUBLISHING, Buderim, Queensland, Australia*

© Copyright [2025] LYDIA–JANE PLANTE – All rights reserved.

ISBN: 978-1-7636729-0-1

The contents of this book may not be reproduced, duplicated, or transmitted without direct written permission from the author.

Under no circumstances will any legal responsibility or blame be held against the publisher for any reparation, damages, or monetary loss due to the information herein, either directly or indirectly.

Legal Notice:

This book is copyright-protected. This is only for personal use. You cannot amend, distribute, sell, use, quote, or paraphrase any part of the content within this book without the consent of the author.

Disclaimer Notice:

Please note the information contained within this document is for educational and entertainment purposes only. Every attempt has been made to provide accurate, up-to- date, and reliable complete information. No warranties of any kind are expressed or implied. Readers acknowledge that the author is not engaging in the rendering of legal, financial, medical, or professional advice. The content of this book has been derived from various sources. By reading this document, the reader agrees that under no circumstances is the author responsible for any losses, direct or indirect, which are incurred as a result of the use of information contained within this document, including, but not limited to, errors, omissions, or inaccuracies.

Author's Note

Many of the references cited for this book have come from Wikipedia which is not a primary source and can be easily edited and changed. However, since this is not intended to be an academic work, the use of secondary sources is, I believe, quite acceptable for a book of this type. I have used links to the actual pages cited, so in many cases, if accessed, the reference will be referred to as an "older" reference. In many instances, Wikipedia cites primary sources which can be accessed by interested parties.

Dedication

This book is dedicated to my mother, Violet, who loved all things to do with Robin Hood, especially Maid Marian.

Table of Contents

Introduction 1

Chapter One   3

   Folklore, Myth, and Legend 3
   The Legend of Marian 5

Chapter Two   9

   Maid Marian of Sherwood Forest 9

Chapter Three   17

   Maid Marian and George-a-Green 17
   Maid Marian and The Witch of Paplewick 20
   Maid Marian – Wed at Last Then Widowed 22

Chapter Four   27

   Maid Marian's Earliest Forms 27
   Maid Marian as a Medieval Literary Character 30
   The Different Faces of Maid Marian 36

Chapter five   39

   The Tale of Robert, Baron Fitzwalter 39
   The Legend of Lady Matilda Fitzwalter 41

Chapter Six   45

   Anthony Munday's Robin Hood Plays 45
   The Death of Robert, Earl of Huntingdon 50

Chapter Seven   53

   About Robin Hood 53
   The First Appearance of Robin Hood in Text 55
   Maid Marian and Friar Tuck Join the Narrative 57

Chapter Eight	59
Thomas Love Peacock's Maid Marian	60
Chapter Nine	69
More Maid Marian texts of the 19th Century	69
Chapter Ten	75
Maid Marian in 20th Century Literature	75
Chapter Eleven	83
Maid Marian in 21st Century Literature	83
Gender-Swapping Robin Hood	88
Chapter Twelve	91
Maid Marian in Opera	91
Chapter Thirteen	97
Maid Marian in the Movies	97
The First Major Robin Hood Movie	97
Chapter Fourteen	103
The Adventures of Robin Hood	103
Chapter Fifteen	111
Maid Marian Screen Depictions in the 1950s, 60s, and 70s	111
Maid Marian Depictions in the 1990s, 2000s, and to the Present	114
Chapter Sixteen	125
Maid Marian on Television	125
Animated Series Featuring Maid Marian	131
Chapter Seventeen - Conclusion	133
Bibliography	135
About the Author	149

INTRODUCTION

"History belongs to the victors, legends to the people, fantasy to literature..." – Péter Esterházy (Good Reads, 2023)

Over the centuries, there has been an age-old story told and retold countless times; the tale of Robin Hood—the skillful archer who gallivanted through Sherwood Forest stealing from the corrupt rich to give to the starving poor during medieval times. But what of the woman whose tale was so often overshadowed by that of her outlaw lover and husband, Maid Marian?

In truth, Marian was so much more than just Robin's love interest or even his damsel in distress. She evolved from ballad and poem through history to stage and screen in modern times. Her medieval incarnation as shepherdess or noblewoman developed into her modern-day portrayal as an empowered woman standing shoulder to shoulder with Robin Hood himself. Her character serves not only as a romantic counterpart but represents strength and resilience against adversity, resonating deeply within our collective psyche.

But Lady Marian, as she is also called, is far more than a Lois Lane figure to Robin Hood's Superman. She is a fully fleshed-out character in her own right, with her own skills, traits, and motivations. Her first appearances in literature were not even in the *Robin Hood* stories and Maid Marian's evolution through history is even more fascinating than that of the outlaw hero.

From the early ballads featuring her to the real woman who inspired the fictional version of her, the origins of Maid Marian were a solid foundation from which to grow. She has been through a tremendous transformation through the ages, depending on who decided to tell her tale. Indeed, there have been countless iterations of her seen in literature, films and television over many years.

Maid Marian has taken on various roles during different eras in history, reflecting the changing attitudes of women in society. This makes her so much more than a fictional character. She transcends the purpose of just being a love interest to a folk hero—instead, she is a meaningful symbol of female empowerment and gender equality. Her journey from a shepherdess to a skilled archer who could rival any of the merry men in competitions is a vital chapter in women's literary history.

At times, Maid Marian may have been seen as nothing but a damsel in distress of Middle-Age Europe, but more frequently, her character has been one of strength and fortitude. It is no wonder she has become an internationally recognized figure, inspiring artists, historians, writers, poets and filmmakers the world over for centuries.

The sheer prevalence of Maid Marian in pop culture is a testament to her contribution to human society. Today, she continues to make appearances in novels and every other form of media as well, lengthening her legacy as one of the most prominent figures of legend that there has ever been.

Chapter One

Maid Marian—the epitome of strong, loyal, and loving femininity—has been inspiring the imagination of writers and artists for around 700 years. Though she is often linked with Robin Hood, thanks to several early authors she has been reclaimed as a feminist icon in more modern literature.

To understand the path that Maid Marian has taken throughout her journey as a character, we need to look at her origins in British folklore. For this, let us first examine just what folklore is and how its subcategories differ from each other.

Folklore, Myth, and Legend

The folklore of any group of people is an important part of their culture. Stories, songs, proverbs, and superstitions are all considered folklore, as are the customs, music, dance, festivals and even the traditional costumes of a group of people. In many ways, sharing the same folklore is what defines cultural identity.

Johann Gottfried von Herder was an 18th century philosopher and theologian who became interested in collecting the tales, traditions and songs of Germanic people (Wikipedia, 2023h). He put forward various "authentic" conceptions of *Volk* ("folk, nation, populace" in English) together with the unity of the individual and natural law. He maintained that "there is only one class in the state, the *Volk*," a class that included the king as well as the peasant, so that the *Volk* was not the rabble but was the emergence of "the people" as a basis for the emergence of a classless but hierarchical national body. Yet it was William John Thoms (Liberman, 2008), an English antiquarian using the pseudonym Ambrose Merton, who coined the English word "folklore—the lore of the people" in 1846, spawning an interest in collecting the stories that had been told for generations.

Most folk tales were, at least originally, passed by word of mouth. This is called oral tradition and more often than not, these stories were more than just entertaining narratives told to pass the time. Rather, the tales typically contained some lesson or cultural truth that was embedded in story form so that it could be easily remembered. This is the same reason that so many of them are told in song—especially ballads and rhymes.

Folklore is such a meaningful part of the human experience that the tales from long ago often survive for many generations. Not only that, but they inspire their descendants who put new twists on them and keep them in the consciousness of people of every era. Disney movies are famous for producing their versions of old fairy tales, some of which have existed for millennia.

Fairy tales encompass the type of folklore that has magical or supernatural elements. Two other specific forms of folklore are myths and legends. What is the difference between the two? Myths are often attempts to explain why the world is the way it is. For instance, creation myths are about how the universe came into being. Other themes may be how animals came to look as they do or how humans discovered fire. The ancient Greek myth of Pandora's box (or jar in some versions) is one that explains how evil and suffering were released into the world (Greek Mythology, n.d.).

Many myths include gods, spirits, or deities as characters, together with hero figures who may or may not have been divine. Some popular examples from literature are the myths of Hercules from Ancient Greece and the myth of the Norse god Odin losing his eye to gain knowledge (Historiska, 2023).

Legends have a lot of similar elements to myths. For instance, many legends are about heroes. Sometimes, these heroes are based on actual people from history. Their stories are told and retold, with embellishments and exaggerations being added over time.

Chapter One

In North America, there is the legend of John Henry, an African-American steel driver who beat a steam-powered machine at drilling steel, although it cost him his life (Britannica, 2020). One of the most famous legends to come out of England is the tale of King Arthur and his Knights of the Round Table. His story has been told in many different variations over the centuries, together with all the characters associated with him, for example, Guinevere, Lancelot, Merlin, and Morgan Le Fay (King Arthur's Knights, 2022).

King Arthur ruled over Camelot, which itself has become legendary. In fact, places are very significant aspects of legends. In some of them, places are actually considered as main characters. Examples that come to mind are Atlantis, Shangri-La, or Sherwood Forest.

Yes, Robin Hood's haunt of Sherwood Forest is a crucial part of his tale, and, by association, the tale of Maid Marian—for she is indeed a true heroine of legend, inspired by a real woman who once lived. Though her roots are deeper than most people realize, we should first refer to the most popular version of her story that has prevailed throughout history.

THE LEGEND OF MARIAN

As often happens with myths, legends, and other types of folklore, there are multiple versions of the story of Maid Marian, depending on who decided to write about her. Thus, when talking about these multiple iterations, the names of several characters, including Marian, change depending on the variation they are in. When talking about her in this book, the spelling used is always that used by the author or creator of each iteration.

Marian is most well-known as the lady love of Robin Hood, a medieval outlaw figure who led a band of archers against the corrupt tyrant Prince John. But she was not even a character in the original ballads of Robin Hood—although she still existed. So, who was she before she became Robin Hood's lady love and wife? When did she appear in his tales and how has she enriched the story of the talented archer rogue?

All of this and more will be examined, but firstly, a solid idea must be obtained of some of the most preeminent roles that Maid Marian has played in the tales that so many of us have come to know and love. Since her earliest appearances, she has been described as both beautiful and brave. The *Robin Hood and Maid Marian* Child Ballad 150 (Child, 1888e; Terre Celtiche Blog, 2023), from the 17th century—which we'll revisit in the next chapter—begins:

V. 1	A bonny fine maid of a noble degree,
	With a hey down down a down down
	Maid Marian calld by name,
	Did live in the North, of excellent worth,
	For she was a gallant dame.
V. 2	For favour and face, and beauty most rare,
	Queen Hellen shee did excell;
	For Marian then was praisd of all men
	That did in the country dwell.
V. 3	'Twas neither Rosamond nor Jane Shore,
	Whose beauty was clear and bright,
	That could surpass this country lass,
	Beloved of lord and knight.

This also mentions that she was noble, which is common for her character. Yet, sometimes Marian is described as a Norman heiress and sometimes she is found among the Saxon nobility. Most commonly, she is known as Lady Marian Fitzwalter, a surname probably taken directly from a real woman, Matilda Fitzwalter, whom we will discuss more in a later chapter.

Lady Marian Fitzwalter is how she is known in Roger Lancelyn Green's *The Adventures of Robin Hood*, the quintessential classic first published in 1956 (Green, 2010). This is one of the best-loved versions of the legend and is the one that many people who discovered Robin Hood in their childhood are most familiar with today.

It was Green who took up the task of combing through the old ballads, poems, and plays to compile his masterful retelling of the legendary figures to delight young readers. He was inspired by the stories at an early age when frequent illnesses required him to stay at home and do little but read.

As an adult, Green studied under C.S. Lewis at Merton College, Oxford, obtaining a Bachelor of Letters (B. Litt) degree. During his time as an undergraduate he performed in the Oxford University Dramatic Society's Shakespeare dramas, and he was deputy librarian at Merton College from 1945 to 1950 (The Silent Planet Wiki, n.d.).

Several of Green's retellings of traditional tales have reached the status of classics, including *The Adventures of Robin Hood*. Once it was published, future variations of Robin Hood tended to rely heavily on this work, since Green had taken a rather confusing and complex mass of the older texts about the character and weaved them into a chronological and compelling story that enchanted readers, no matter their age. So, let us explore his iteration of Lady Marian as a brave and chaste heroine, and later, we will revisit Green again when we discuss Robin Hood himself.

At the beginning of *The Adventures of Robin Hood*, our main character was born Robert Fitzooth who became the Earl of Huntingdon. On the eve of his wedding to Lady Marian, daughter of Lord Fitzwalter, he threw a feast. Prince John and the Sheriff of Nottingham arrived in disguise, and it was revealed to them that Robert Fitzooth was Robin Hood, a supposed traitor who undermined Prince John's authority.

After this, our villainous prince made a plan. He was going to declare Robert an outlaw on his wedding day and seize his lands and coffers of gold. But that was not all. In addition, he decided that he would give Lady Marian to Sir Guy of Gisborne, whom he was certain would pay him handsomely for such a fine and noble bride.

On the wedding day, "before ever the words were spoken which would make Robert and Marian man and wife," a knight strode up to the chapel with a band of armed men behind him and forbade the ceremony to continue. After Robert was exposed as Robin Hood and charged with being a traitor who had broken the King's Laws, he gave in, but not before first asking Lady Marian if she gave her love to him as the Earl or to "plain Robin Hood the outlaw."

Lady Marian affirmed that "neither to the Earl nor to his Earldom, but to the man whom I love and whose wife alone I shall be." Robin Hood said that even though the ceremony was only half completed, he considered them to be "man and wife in the sight of God." With that he entrusted Lord Fitzwalter to care for her and protect her until King Richard returned to complete the marriage.

Before Robin Hood fled into the forest, Lady Marian cried, "You, Robin, are my lord and my husband and no other shall ever be aught to me, though I live and die a maid!"

The next morning, Friar Tuck, another staple character in the legend, rode with Sir Guy of Gisborne to Arlingford Castle where Lord Fitzwalter and Lady Marian resided. On the way, the friar warned Sir Guy that "Lady Marian is as apt with an arrow as most damsels are with a needle!" but all Sir Guy could focus on was Lord Fitzwalter's rage at how his daughter's betrothed had proved to be the outlaw, Robin Hood.

When Lady Marian came down, "clad in Lincoln green, with a quiver of arrows at her side and a bow in her hand," Lord Fitzwalter wanted to know where she was going. "To the greenwood," she told him. Lord Fitzwalter forbade it, but Lady Marian told him she would go anyway, and he grew more furious.

Sir Guy mentioned that a husband would be "the best curb" for such a "wayward girl" and Lord Fitzwalter looked at him approvingly. But Lady Marian would not stand to be left out of the conversation about her own life. She said that no man chosen for her as a husband would do, "unless he be my choice also. And my choice is and will ever be for brave Robin Hood!"

While Lord Fitzwalter roared at her disobedience, she softened a little, telling him that she would return. "And I promise also that Robin shall be nothing more to me than he is now, without your leave—or until King Richard return and give me to him in marriage with his own hand." Then she blew him a kiss, ignored Sir Guy completely, and left.

Lady Marian reappeared a few chapters later, where her character was fleshed out and she became the woman who has since earned legendary status.

Chapter Two

Maid Marian of Sherwood Forest

The seventh chapter of Green's book is titled *Maid Marian of Sherwood Forest*. In it, Green tells how Sir William Gamwell, who was Robin Hood's uncle in this version, was going to hold a "great Gamwell festival" in the forest near his home of Gamwell Hall. He invited Sir Guy of Gisborne—one of Robin Hood's arch nemeses. Sir Guy agreed to attend in the hopes of finding out where Robin Hood was hiding.

The day arrived and was "a merry scene in the green glade of the forest: young men and girls dancing round the Maypole, barrels of ale broached for Sir William's tenants and many a game or contest for young and old alike." Sir Guy and his squire sat with Sir William under a tree observing the festivities, when suddenly, Sir Guy leant forward.

"With an angry glint in his eyes," he stared at Sir William's son, who had on his arm a maiden whom Sir Guy thought he had seen before. Even though she was dressed as a peasant, he indeed recognized the young woman. She was none other than Lady Marian Fitzwalter!

But when Sir Guy asked Sir William with whom his son was dancing, Sir William replied, "Oh, she is known as the shepherdess Clorinda: she is often at these feasts but really I can tell you little of her!"

Sir Guy thought to himself, "You mean you won't tell me!"

A little later, a "band of foresters" arrived and began to engage in an archery contest. Clorinda joined them and "seemed as good an archer as any of them." Sir Guy rode closer to the contest and watched her shoot an arrow straight into the center of the target. That was when a strapping young man who appeared to be "chief" among the foresters stepped forward.

"I must needs shoot well indeed to equal that, fair Clorinda," he said. And he proceeded to prove his declaration true. Everyone cheered as his arrow struck so close to Clorinda's that "the points were in contact and the feathers were intermingled." This appeared to be a nice bit of foreshadowing and maybe even held a little innuendo.

Green also called back to Lady Marian's roots when he had the archer bow before her and say, "I claim your hand, fair Queen of the May." She blushed and smiled and allowed him to lead her into a dance, while Sir Guy put two and two together and realized that the man was the outlaw he had been looking for.

As before, he decided he needed confirmation, so he asked Sir William's son the identity of the man. Young Gamwell tried to be dismissive, but Sir Guy revealed that he knew the archer to be Robert Fitzooth, the Earl of Huntingdon—this was one of Robin Hood's more prominent original names. Sir Guy also stated that there was a large reward for his capture. He wanted to seize the archer and take him immediately to the Sheriff of Nottingham.

He questioned Gamwell as to what might happen if he attempted to capture Robin Hood, and Gamwell gave Sir Guy this warning: "I would advise you

Chapter Two

to turn around and ride your hardest for Nottingham—unless you want a volley of arrows, a shower of stones, and a hailstorm of cudgel-blows to help you on your way!"

Hearing this, Sir Guy's squire left hurriedly, and Sir Guy, not willing to try anything on his own, rushed after him. They immediately made their way to Nottingham to rouse the sheriff, then hurried back to the glade with a troupe of armed men. Whom should they come upon first? Why, our courageous Lady Marian, still in disguise.

Sir Guy, the Sheriff of Nottingham, and their band came to a bridge and encountered "a small party of foresters and men at arms headed by the shepherdess Clorinda who still carried her bow." By her side stood the big Friar Tuck.

They reached the bridge first and Sir Guy bellowed, "Out of the way, renegade Friar! And you, Lady Marian, hasten away to Arlingford, for you are in truly doubtful and traitorous company."

"You mistake, false knight, you mistake!" declared Friar Tuck. "The lady here is the fair Clorinda, well known throughout the forest of Sherwood as the Queen of the Shepherdesses. As for the doubtful and traitorous company—I see none of it on *this* side of the bridge!"

This angered the sheriff greatly and he shouted at them to move aside so they could continue their search for Robin Hood. Friar Tuck refused, telling them that they would not be able to pass by on the bridge "until you have made full apology to the fair Clorinda and myself for all terms, taunts, and other words of slander uttered in the hearing of these good fellows!"

Sir Guy interjected again, demanding that his men "force them aside!" He also raised his hand in the air and said, "And catch that forward girl for me: Lord Fitzwalter will reward me well when I bring her back to him!"

Well, Lady Marian was going to have none of that. "Swift as thought Clorinda raised her bow, the string hummed, and Sir Guy's hand was transfixed by an arrow." In other words, his palm had just been pierced.

The sheriff ordered his men to "cut them down" but that was when "the bowstring hummed again, the sheriff's horse reared up as an arrow whizzed into the ground between its forefeet, and the sheriff fell backwards out of the saddle and sat heavily down in a large pool of mud." A brief battle ensued, but inevitably ended with the sheriff and Sir Guy fleeing for their lives as the fair 'Clorinda' laughed and Friar Tuck jeered at them.

Then there was a break in the story and the narrative moved forward to the next morning at Fitzwalter castle. Lord Fitzwalter's breakfast was disturbed by a trumpet blast, and when he went to see why an alarm had been raised, he spied a large group of armed men who commanded him to lower his drawbridge.

Lady Marian must have inherited some of her courage from her father, for he demanded of them immediately why he should agree to such an order. The herald in the group of men said that the Sheriff of Nottingham and Sir Guy of Gisborne were recovering from wounds and that Lady Marian Fitzwalter was charged, together with Gamwell and Friar Tuck, "as agents and accomplices in the said riot, and traitors for that they have aided and consorted with the outlaw Robin Hood."

Lord Fitzwalter was flabbergasted, but he had a good head on his shoulders. "What do you mean by coming here with this nonsensical story of my daughter, the Lady Marian, bruising the sheriff, injuring his men and shooting arrows into Sir Guy of Gisborne!" he said. Then he bade them to be off, but the troop reminded him that their lord was Prince John, and that Lord Fitzwalter should not go against his wishes.

However, the shrewd Lord Fitzwalter still did not back down. He addressed the men saying, "Then let him come in person or send someone whom I can trust. How know I that you are not some of these very Sherwood outlaws in disguise, trying to gain entrance to my castle under cover of the King's name and a silly story about my girl bruising sheriffs and shooting men-at-arms!"

Once the troop left with promises to return, Lord Fitzwalter called for his daughter. When he demanded the truth from her, Lady Marian confessed and Lord Fitzwalter told her, "You go no more forth from the castle!"

Lady Marian, displaying another trait she perhaps inherited from him, was defiant. "Then I get out if I can and am under no obligation to return." Lord Fitzwalter told her to go to the "topmost turret chamber" where no one would get to her, but Lady Marian reminded him that Prince John could get to her. She said, "He saw me on the eve of my wedding to Robin of Locksley, and it is said that he has sworn to take me and perhaps not hand me over to Sir Guy as readily as he has promised."

Lord Fitzwalter claimed he would "defy a wicked Prince as surely as a wicked knight" but Lady Marian insisted that Prince John commanded much more power and would sack the castle to get to her. "But if you shut me up—and I escape from the castle, no blame can be attached to you, and you can welcome him here with every sign of regret for my absence and fury at my flight."

Realizing the wisdom of his daughter's words, Lord Fitzwalter decided that was what must be done. But he was still concerned about her: "Do you go to Sherwood Forest as half wife of this outlaw Robin Hood?"

She confirmed that she would, "but until King Richard returns from Palestine, pardons him [Robin Hood] and restores him to his rightful position, I dwell in Sherwood Forest as Maid Marian promised—but not united to Robin. And this he has sworn by God and Our Lady, and here and now I re-affirm the oath."

Lord Fitzwalter decided that Robin was an honorable man, and he trusted that Lady Marian would bring no dishonor to the family. So, he relented and agreed to her plan bidding her to go to her room and not let anyone see her when she left the castle.

After a few hours, Prince John rode up "at the head of a hundred men" and Lord Fitzwalter greeted him warmly. He apologized for his earlier behavior but said he could not trust anyone whilst the outlaw was on the loose. He also placed his entire castle at the disposal of Prince John, who was happy to be treated so graciously.

But when Prince John asked to see Lady Marian, it was discovered her room was empty. Employing his acting talents again, Lord Fitzwalter flew into a rage and cursed the carelessness of the castle guards. He then sent some of them to search the neighborhood with Prince John's men, but everyone was soon in agreement that "Lady Marian Fitzwalter had vanished."

Meanwhile, Robin Hood had disguised himself as a forest ranger to meet with any travelers who might have had news about Prince John and his intentions. Soon he spotted a young man with a bow and arrows, as well as a broadsword, hustling down the road. Robin Hood stopped him and asked him about the news of Nottingham that day. The youth told him that Prince John had arrived in Nottingham to "put down the outlaws in the forest."

At that point Robin Hood inquired about the youth's identity: "Tell me your name and business, or my sword must enforce it," he demanded.

But the young man cried, "Two can play at that game," and dropped his bow and arrows, and promptly pulled out his sword. Robin Hood followed suit and quite quickly realized "his antagonist was at least his match in all the skill and practice of swordsmanship, though weaker in the wrist than he, and not so heavy in the sheer weight of blows."

The two of them fought for some time and even wounded each other, until finally, Robin Hood stepped back and leant on his sword. He completely forgot that he was pretending to be a forest ranger and said, "You fight too well to be wasted like this: come, throw in your lot with Robin Hood and be one of his merry men."

The youth seemed surprised: "Are you Robin Hood?"

"Robin Hood I am, and no other!" replied the man.

"'Oh, Robin, Robin! Do you not know me?' cried his late antagonist with a sudden change of voice."

And by now, I'm sure you know who our sword-wielding youth really was.

"'Marian!' gasped Robin. 'And I wounded you, and knew you not!' And a moment later he wrapped her in his arms—a perfect example of the drama and convenient coincidences of these old tales.

Robin Hood bade Lady Marian to come with him once she told him of her woes, and he promised that his men would "welcome their queen—as I do; and swear, as I do, to be true and faithful servants now and henceforward to you, Maid Marian of Sherwood Forest."

He made good on his promise. During an evening of feasting, Robin Hood asked everyone to "drink to our Maiden Queen! To the Lady Marian!" He continued with a poignant decree: "Let us pledge ourselves once more to the true service of God and His Holy Mother, as true Christian men should. But let us also even as true knights to their lady, pledge ourselves that all our actions shall be so pure and so far from all evil that we do nothing we should think shame of it were it done in the presence of our queen, our Maid Marian!" And all the men enthusiastically shouted their agreement and drank a toast to Robin Hood and Maid Marian.

After this exciting part, Lady Marian made only a few brief appearances in the narrative until closer to the end. For all the descriptions of her fighting skills, she did not join Robin Hood and his merry men in their antics for a considerable time. The way Robin Hood was characterized, it was likely that he wanted to keep her as safe as possible. But she reappeared in some key parts in the last handful of chapters.

Chapter Three

Maid Marian and George-a-Green

George-a-Green, *the Pinner of Wakefield*, the 16th chapter of Roger Lancelyn Green's book, is based on a few scenes in a play with the same name and first performed in 1593 and published in a 1599 Quarto (Anonymous, 2021). The story outlines how a new medieval champion and his lady love were suddenly becoming famous and overshadowing Maid Marian and Robin Hood. This appears to be a few years after Marian fled her home to go and live in the forest and she seemed somewhat put out by this development.

Robin Hood saw her being melancholy while they "sat near to one another by the great trysting tree in the secret glade" and asked her what was wrong.

" 'You must not laugh at me, Robin,' she said, looking half-ashamed as she spoke. 'I think these long days of wet spring after snowy winter when there is little I can do—I think they are largely to blame: surely otherwise, I would not worry about so trifling a care.' "

To which Robin Hood replied, "Dear heart, you know well that no care of yours can seem a trifle to me. Tell on, I pray you."

Then, in a strange and almost uncharacteristic way, Marian described how she was hearing more and more of "the deeds and the valour of this George-a-Greene, and of the beauty of his love the fair Bettris who is said to exceed all women in her loveliness." Marian was depicted as almost jealous, or at the very least, petulant. "Until lately, your name, my Robin, was on everyone's lips and in all the songs of the minstrels and pedlars, and they told of your deeds of prowess, your skill with bow or with quarter-staff, and—and of Maid Marian the Queen of Sherwood."

Robin Hood was quick to dismiss her concern, telling her that George-a-Greene "is an upstart and rides to fame on a bubble reputation which will burst sooner or later" and that "as for this Bettris of his, I'll wager my head that could you but be seen once in her company, no one would look at her again!"

Then Marian slyly suggested that they go to Wakefield as she could not bear the thought of people thinking that George-a-Greene could defeat Robin Hood with the quarter-staff. So off they went, with Marian disguised as a forester.

Once they came upon George-a-Greene, the two of them fought but soon saw they were so equally matched, that they ceased. Robin Hood asked George to leave Wakefield and join his band in Sherwood Forest, and George consented, asking if his dear love Bettris would also be welcomed. That's when Robin Hood presented Maid Marian, and George and Bettris exclaimed in surprise.

"When she [Maid Marian] flung her hood and let the loveliness of her hair come tumbling all about her face, no one could doubt that she was far [*sic*] the loveliest lady in all the North Country, and Bettris, though comely and winsome, could never compare with her." But the two women bonded immediately and Bettris was only too eager to don men's clothing as she and her betrothed joined the group.

In the following chapter, they made their way from Wakefield to Sherwood when they decided to pay a visit to Allin-a-Dale and his wife. Since there was a rainstorm, they sought shelter but feared that they were being followed by rogues and thus bringing danger with them. However, Allin-a-Dale welcomed them all inside.

Shortly afterward, someone knocked on the door also asking for shelter from the nasty weather. But Robin Hood, George, and the rest were not tricked. While the men lined up and strung their bows, Marian "without a moment's hesitation took her stand beside Robin and made ready her bow also. But Bettris and Allin's wife armed themselves with spits as long and as sharp as javelins or short throwing spears and took their stands on either side of the doorway."

The gang of rogues crashed through the door, but Robin and his friends were all ready for the group, who proved to be a bunch of knights. The fight was chaotic, with Marian putting an end to it when she leapt forward to meet with one of the knights, "parried his blow so dextrously that the sword flew from his hand, and a moment later a well-aimed kettle hurled by Bettris laid him on the floor." Maid Marian then proceeded to straddle him and push the point of her sword into his face, threatening to slay him if his men did not cease their combat.

Once the knight spoke, Marian recognized him as Sir Guy of Gisborne, and she flung back her hood so he could see who had just defeated him. Sir Guy claimed, "only for love of you have I sought so hard and so often to take you from Robin Hood."

Marian was disgusted. She told him, "Many times you have sought the life of my lord—and of me as well, for I could not live were Robin no more. And do you think me so spiritless as to believe that I could be yours by compulsion? You know well that I would die rather than that—and death is easy to find."

Robin Hood wanted to strike off Sir Guy's head, but Marian said no, and instead made him swear an oath: "Sir Guy, you shall swear by the oath that you hold most sacred, first that you will seek no vengeance on these good people who shielded us and helped us against you; and second, never more to pursue my lord Robin Hood or me—and on these conditions you shall live."

Sir Guy of Gisborne swore the oath and left with his men. George-a-Greene was delighted with the action and even more eager to join the merry men. Bettris agreed, with one caveat. "I would I could wield a sword as well as Maid Marian. George, you have failed in your duties towards me!"

" 'By not teaching my wife to fight?' laughed George. 'By Our Lady, no court in Christendom would accept that as a cause of complaint.' " The chapter ended happily, and Robin Hood and his group embarked on "one of the strangest adventures that ever befell them" in the next section.

Maid Marian and The Witch of Paplewick

For this tale, Green was inspired by the play *The Sad Shepherd: or, A Tale of Robin Hood* written by Ben Jonson in the 1600s (Fortunaso, 1641; Jonson, 1905). The play was left incomplete upon Jonson's death and an ending was tacked on some centuries later by Francis Godolphin Waldron (Dobson & Taylor, 1989b). Green didn't approve of this ending, so he wrote his own when retelling the story in his book.

At the start of *The Witch of Paplewick*, (sometimes written as *Papplewick*) Maid Marian returned to the camp after having just taken down a deer to cook for their dinner. She proclaimed, "Robin, my love! Oh, now my day's happiness is complete! I rose early, early before the sun, and such fine sport we had seeking the deer. Then one shot brought him down, a long shot, and my arrow in his heart."

Then she remarked that "one shadow" did fall upon them while they were out hunting. It was when they had been cutting up the deer carcass to bring it back that "a raven sat upon the tree over our heads and croaked dismally."

Chapter Three

Robin Hood laughed this off until Marian said a shepherd whom they met told them the raven was Mother Maudlin, the Witch of Paplewick, who could take any form she wanted. And that Maudlin had told the shepherd "Ill things would this day befall any who ate of the deer at Robin Hood's feast!"

Green let us know that "indeed at that time all men believed in witchcraft—and doubtless that was why there were then still witches to be found who were indeed in touch with the darker powers of evil."

So, Marian went to wash in the stream, and when she came back, she was entirely changed. She snapped at Robin Hood, telling him that his band "shall not feast on this venison! It is too good for such course [*sic*], rustic mouths that cannot open to thank for it." Then, she commanded Will Scarlet to take the meat to Mother Maudlin, "the wise woman you call a witch" because she would at least be grateful.

Robin Hood thought that his love had become ill, especially when she told him, "You it is who spy on everything I do, and follow me everywhere with your jealousy and oppression" and then stamped away. Confused, Robin Hood followed her only to find her sitting idly by the stream listening to a shepherdess tell of the woes of Eglamour, who had lost his love, Earine.

Maid Marian jumped up and ran to him when she saw him, but Robin Hood was puzzled and questioned her about her earlier behavior. She had no recollection of it and told him she had just come to wash in the stream when she found the shepherdess and was listening to what happened to Eglamour. The shepherdess herself confirmed this was true.

But Will Scarlet had already taken the venison to Mother Maudlin. He was told to go and retrieve it. As they were all trying to puzzle out what had happened, Maudlin herself appeared—as an old woman—to thank Marian for the gift. But she denied that she had ever ordered anyone to send the deer to her.

In the meantime, Will Scarlet arrived and told them that he had brought the venison back and Maudlin cried, "Do you give a thing, and then take it back again?" She cursed them all and rushed away, but not before putting a spell on their cook, who was soon doubled over in pain.

Robin Hood went after her, and when he came upon Mother Maudlin's house, she was disguised as Maid Marian again. At that point he saw that she was wearing a girdle decorated with mystical signs. Robin Hood ripped it off her and threw it into the water while Maudlin fumed with rage. He told her to leave immediately, or his men would hunt her "like a wolf."

After Mother Maudlin fled, Robin Hood set fire to her house, and she was never seen in Sherwood Forest again. This scene is just one example of a "false Marian" story, in which a character with malicious intentions pretends to be the lady we know to be pure and good-hearted.

Maid Marian – Wed at Last Then Widowed

In Chapter 21 in *The Adventures of Robin Hood*, we find Lady Marian sitting with Bettris by a cave, "lashing the grey goose feathers onto arrow-shafts while the morning stole on to noon." Their work was rudely interrupted by Prince John and a small band of armed men.

"So, here's the tigress in her den!" Prince John cried. "At last, Marian, after all these years, we meet again—and not to part so speedily as last time." But before he could lay a hand on her, Marian pulled her horn from her belt and blew into it. Bettris then handed her a sword and she stood defensively before the prince.

After scolding his men for not capturing her, Prince John commanded them to grab her. Maid Marian "disarmed one with a quick turn of her wrist, and then after a few moments of desperate swordplay laid the other dead on

Chapter Three

the ground." But even with Bettris' help, she was no match for so many and they quickly overpowered her.

Prince John insulted her, and Maid Marian struck him across the face. He raised his hand to give it back to her but was stabbed between the thumb and his pointer finger by an arrow. Robin Hood challenged him to a sword fight, but Prince John ordered his men to fight instead. As some of the Sherwood Forest band emerged from the trees and restrained the prince, Robin Hood quickly took out one of the guards. The others turned and ran, only to be shot and killed by the arrows before they could escape.

A "tall palmer" soon joined the foresters and Robin Hood explained to him who he and his merry men were and all they had done. Afterward, they brought their prisoner Prince John out who turned a "ghastly colour" when he saw the palmer's face, for it was his older brother, King Richard!

The outlaws all bowed before the rightful monarch, but King Richard told them to stand. Then, he pardoned them all and asked Robin, "I have heard said—for you and your doings are spoken of throughout England—that the Lady Marian lives still a maid until I, the King, return to give her hand to you in marriage. Is this true?"

"'It is, my liege,' answered Robin, and Marian came and stood beside him and slipped her hand into his."

"Then here and now I give her to you," the King replied and called upon the Bishop of Hereford, who was also present, to join their hands in holy matrimony with Friar Tuck acting as clerk for him. "So Robin Hood and Maid Marian were wedded there in Sherwood Forest, with Richard Cœur de Lion to give the bride away. And after that they set forward for Nottingham in triumph, Richard riding at the head of them all, with Marian at his side and Robin beyond her."

You would think that would be the end, but there was more to come. Robin Hood and Lady Marian "lived quietly at Locksley" for five years, during which time King Richard went to war again, taking some of Robin Hood's old band with him. When rumors began circulating about Prince John and the Sheriff of Nottingham being spotted together again, Robin Hood found it difficult to believe.

He went into town to attend Mass, leaving some men to guard the Lady Marian, and he was promptly seized by the sheriff. When Robin Hood was brought before Prince John, he learned that King Richard had died, and the dastardly John was now the king. "When you are dead there will be no one to stand between me and Lady Marian— as you stood that day in Sherwood Forest," the new king told him. Then, he bound Robin Hood against the wall and left.

It took several hours and the help of Little John, who shot an arrow through the window with a sturdy rope, but Robin Hood managed to escape. He rushed to Locksley and retrieved Lady Marian, and they slipped into the forest with the King's guard on their heels. After killing the Sheriff of Nottingham, Robin Hood told Lady Marian to seek sanctuary in a nearby nunnery. She did not want to go without him, but he insisted, and they parted with a sweet kiss.

Once she was there, the Prioress spent many days trying to convince Lady Marian that Robin Hood was dead. She wanted Lady Marian to take her vows and become a nun so that she would truly be safe from King John. In reality she wanted the Locksley estate to come under the control of the nunnery. Finally, Lady Marian gave in.

Eventually, a very weak and wounded Robin Hood arrived at the nunnery, and the Prioress tended to his wounds. She also lied and told him that Lady Marian had returned to Locksley. And once she learned Robin's real identity, she unfastened the bandage on his arm so that his blood flowed freely, and he grew even weaker. With all the remaining strength he had, he pulled out his bugle and blew it.

Lady Marian heard the call, and she began searching for her beloved, finding him near death. In a bittersweet ending, Robin Hood declared to her, "Here I have come to die and where else could I ask to die but in your arms." Then he shot one last arrow through the window, wishing to be buried where it fell. His wishes were heeded.

Lady Marian stayed on at the nunnery, where it did not take long for her to become the new Prioress, using the name Matilda. "And of the goodness of the Prioress Matilda and of how she was ever ready to help the sick and the afflicted many tales were told." When she died in the same room where Robin Hood had given his last breath, she was then buried next to him, under the greenwood tree.

What a rich, vibrant character she was. As you can see from Roger Lancelyn Green's version, Lady Marian was no passive love interest. She was a skilled archer and fighter, unafraid to stand up to villains, and the foresters were sometimes described as "her followers."

She may have been a "forward girl" as Sir Guy called her, but that kind of woman is the most interesting—someone with spirit and the boldness to fight for what is right. Beyond that, she was ever faithful to the man she loved, as well as to her religion. She cared deeply about those who were wronged or who had come across some ill fortune.

Perhaps most impressively, although she had come from a background of means, she lived in Sherwood Forest for years as the only woman amongst a group of outlawed men. That in itself takes a lot of strength.

But although this variant of her is among the most common, Maid Marian existed as a character outside the Robin Hood legends long before the first was ever written down. In fact, she was linked with a very different type of man, also named Robin, in her earliest incarnations.

Chapter Four

Previous chapters discussed the major interpretation of Maid Marian with which most people today are familiar. However, going even further back in time, before Roger Lancelyn Green's stories, it is evident that Maid Marian's name had already been mentioned.

Maid Marian's Earliest Forms

As far back as we can go with any degree of certainty, the Marian we first encounter may have come from a pagan goddess of the spring. However, it has also been speculated that she was linked with the Virgin Mary, to whom Robin Hood was very devoted (as described in the oldest ballads about him).

In *Brewer's Dictionary of Phrase & Fable* (Brewer, 1993), the entry under "Maid Marian" on page 795 says, "A morris dance, or the boy in the morris dance, was called *Mad Morion,* from the 'morion' [a type of helmet] which he wore on his head." Thus, Maid Marian is both a corruption of the words and sex of the participant. *Brewer* then states that etymologists, using the words 'Maid Marian,' "puzzled out" a suitable identity for her, usually considered as being "Matilda, the daughter of Fitz-Walter, baron of Bayard and Dunmow who eloped with Robert Fitz-Ooth, the outlaw and lived with him in Sherwood Forest."

The Morris Dances probably originated in the European Courts of the 15th century, evolving over time. The earliest reference to Morris dancing in Britain was in 1448 (Wikipedia, 2023k). Little is known about the actual dances, although there seem to have been two types of dances; a solo dance and a dance in a circle about a 'maiden' who might have been a man in women's clothing and for whose favors the dancers competed.

Originally military dances of the Moors, they eventually became performances that included characters such as a peasant named Robin and a shepherdess named Marian. Stephen Knight, in his volume *Robin Hood: A Complete Study of the English Outlaw* (Knight, 1994), believes that the name Marian could have been derived from the "Murrian," also known as the "Moorish one." She very likely would have been depicted with a black face.

Other characters who frequently appeared in the Morris dances were the clown Malkin, the fool Bavian, and a dragon and a hobby horse. Most of the dancers wore bells as they scampered around and amused the attendees. Marian was nearly always seen in the company of a friar, who evolved later into Friar Tuck. It has even been interpreted by some that she was the friar's girlfriend.

You might have heard of—or even celebrated—the May Day festival, held on the first day of the month of May. May Day has its origins in the Roman celebration of spring (Chu, n.d.). People would dance and sing through the fields, all in honor of Flora, the goddess of flowers, fertility and spring. The English festivities included dancing around the maypole, lighting bonfires, and choosing the fairest young woman to be crowned as Queen of the May. During this celebration, they would also play sports and games such as archery.

The legend of Robin Hood grew up in plays and ballads and he came to be associated with the May Games and May Day. The earliest remnant of a play is dated 1475 and called *Robin Hood and the Sheriff* (Dobson & Taylor, 1989e). Two other plays that were published were *Robin Hood and the Friar* and *Robin Hood and the Potter* (Dobson & Taylor, 1989c, 1989d). In the plays, several instances of mock combat occurred with Robin fighting various characters by swordplay and with the staff. The plays were often associated with the May Games and were performed during Pentecost. Robin was thus a perfect choice of a fictional figure to be featured in the plays and dances and he was often represented as King of the May or Summer King. It is important to note that he was not an outlaw originally but seemed to have merged with the character of French lyric poetry and other early ballads at some point. Also, all classes participated in this merriment. Robin Hood, even after he became an outlaw hero, was not just a hero for the poor.

Marian appears to have become part of the May Games folklore without reference to Robin Hood. She originally appears in *Le Jeu de Robin et Marion*, a French secular play by Adam de La Halle, discussed further in the next section (Britannica, 2024a). In this play, Robin was a shepherd and Marion his shepherdess. When Marian became part of the May Games stories, she was transformed as Robin Hood's lover. By the end of the 16th century, Marian was firmly established in references to Robin Hood.

That said, the earliest May Games showcasing Robin Hood were probably performed after the first of May as a distinct celebration. Likewise, while sometimes paired together, historians like Stephen Knight believe the Morris Dances were originally separate traditions from the May Day games and that the two had blended together by the latter half of the 16th century (Fortunaso, n.d.-b).

In any event, the case has been made that this is how Marian became Robin Hood's sweetheart and was so powerfully connected to him. One interesting fact about the plays, some of which will be discussed next, is that the character of the feminine Marian was originally portrayed by a young man or boy. Throughout this time, and indeed well into Shakespeare's era, it was common for men to take on the roles of women in performances like the very first ones that depict our heroine.

MAID MARIAN AS A MEDIEVAL LITERARY CHARACTER

As we've established, the earliest renditions of a Marian figure were in plays performed during the festival of May Day. It was highly likely that this Marian was inspired by the character who appeared in many texts of French lyric poetry during the Middle Ages, where her name was sometimes spelled Marot or Mariet. In these poems, she is usually pursued by a lord or other noble, as well as a peasant named Robin.

Around 1282-1283, poet and composer Adam de la Halle collected several of these poems and elaborated upon them. The result of his work culminated in *Le Jeu de Robin et de Marion*, sometimes shortened to *Robin et Marion*, which is considered the first secular play in French with music (Wikipedia, 2023a). Originally performed in Naples for the court of King Charles I, it was a dramatic version of the *pastourelle*, a genre of poem that was popular in medieval France (Collins Dictionary, 2023). A modern recording of the work by Tonus Peregrinus was made in April 2006 (Naxos, 2006).

Typically, *pastourelles* were romances between a knight and a shepherdess, but *Le Jeu de Robin et de Marion* focused more on the shepherdess, Marion, after she spurned the knight and took a lover named Robin. According to Antony Pitts, writing on Adam's work, the shepherdess Marion emerged as a stronger character than Robin Hood as she snubbed the Knight's unwanted overtures and twisted her fiancé Robin "round her ring finger" (Pitts, n.d.). When the knight whisked her away, Robin attempted to rouse his relatives to save her but could not. Eventually, the knight realized that he would never win Marion's heart, so he allowed her to return to her home. She married Robin at the end of the play, during a festival.

The story included many songs of the period and became quite popular. Sometimes in these old French plays, Robin is referred to as *Robin des bois*, meaning "Robin of the woods," but other than that, he shares little resemblance to the outlaw hero who would become Robin Hood and is generally considered a separate figure. Therefore, while this could have inspired later legends of Robin Hood and Maid Marian, there has yet to be found any firm connection to them.

By the time *Le Jeu de Robin et de Marion* was performed annually in the mid-1300s, John Gower wrote *Mirour de L'Omme*, translated to "The Mirror of Mankind" (Gower, 1992). This was an Anglo-Saxon poem originally composed in the French language. It was long and by most standards, complex, presented as a moral treatise about the degeneration of society.

The reason *Mirour* is mentioned here is because it featured two characters named Robin and Marion. They embodied a rustic lifestyle and were probably references to the figures depicted in the May Games. In his treatise, Gower uses them as part of his critical view of the monks who followed Robin instead of the saintlier Augustine.

The character of Marian mostly vanished in literature from this date until the 16th century. However, she may have appeared in a transformation of her character as Marion Braidfute, in *The Acts and Deeds of the Illustrious and Valiant Champion Sir William Wallace, Knight of Ellerslie* which was first written by Henry the Minstrel, also known as Blind Harry, in the year 1361 (The Minstrel Henry aka Blind Harry, 2015). Many scholars believe the writer of this epic, was both influenced by the Robin Hood legend as well as influencing its evolution with this work. When the film *Braveheart* was released, the name of Wallace's wife Marion Braidfute was changed by director and actor Mel Gibson to Murron MacClannough. This was done in order to avoid any confusion that might have occurred in the light of the Robin

Hood legend. (Braveheart Wiki, 2023), however, journalist Scott Wallace has suggested that William Wallace did not actually marry (Wallace, 2017).

In our heroine's next appearance in literature, Marian popped up on stage in *George-a-Greene, the Pinner of Wakefield* (Anonymous, 2021), and in *Edward I, Scene VII (Peele, 2019),* in the late 16th century. But there is no doubt that the most important early text in which she is featured was written in 1598 by Anthony Munday (Munday, 2010).

These will be examined extensively in the next chapter when the real-life woman who became connected with the fictional heroine is considered. Anthony Munday was responsible for many enduring characteristics of the multiple versions of the story that came after his plays. One of the most prominent is his gentrification of Robin Hood. By making him a lord, as Munday did, he of course needed a lady. And this is where Lady Marian and Robin Hood become inseparable in future books and the later films and television shows based upon them.

It was at this point that the "Maid" title seems to have been given to Marian. This was likely to refer to her promise to remain entirely chaste until Robin Hood was pardoned from his outlaw activities when King Richard returned to England. Thus, Maid Marian was further distinguished from her May Games counterpart, where in some of the portrayals, she was quite bawdy.

From this point, her character steadfastly remains one of purity, loyalty, and strength. The ballads that would follow worked together to cement the identity of the woman who became synonymous with feminine grace and courage—an apt companion for a heroic noble.

Indeed, if you asked anyone the identity of Robin Hood's love, surely the only answer would be Maid Marian. However, in the ballad *Robin Hood's Birth, Breeding, Valor, and Marriage,* she was not his sweetheart. This ballad was collected together with thirty others about Robin Hood and printed in the third volume of *The English and Scottish Popular Ballads*, edited by Francis James Child (Child, 1888d). It was also used with a slightly different title in *Robin Hood, His Deeds and Adventures as Recounted in the Old English Ballads,* selected and illustrated by Lucy Fitch Perkins (Perkins, 1906).

In this tale, Robin Hood courted a shepherdess—actually, the queen of shepherdesses—Clorinda. Perhaps Roger Lancelyn Green attempted to reconcile this when he turned Clorinda into one of Maid Marian's aliases. In any case, in the brief play, while Robin Hood was speaking with a yeoman, Clorinda entered and was described in detail:

V. 27	As that word was spoke, Clorinda came by,
	The queen of the shepherds was she;
	And her gown was of velvet as green as the grass,
	And her buskin did reach to her knee.
V. 28	Her gait it was graceful, her body was straight,
	And her countenance free from pride;
	A bow in her hand, and a quiver of arrows
	Hung dangling by her sweet side.
V. 29	Her eyebrows were black, aye, and so was her hair,
	And her skin was as smooth as glass;
	Her visage spoke wisdom, and modesty too;
	Sets with Robin Hood such a lass!

Clorinda then proceeded to take down the largest deer in a herd with her skill as an archer and Robin Hood was thoroughly impressed, claiming he had never seen a woman like her. He invited her back to his camp in the forest, where he promptly got down to the business of proposing.

V. 36	Clorinda said, "Tell me your name, gentle sir"; And he said, "Tis bold Robin Hood: Squire Gamwel's my uncle, but all my delight Is to dwell in the merry Sherwood;"
V. 37	"For 'tis a fine life, and 'tis void of all strife." "So 'tis sir," Clorinda replied. "But oh," said bold Robin, "how sweet would it be, If Clorinda would be my bride!"
V. 38	She blushed at the motion, yet after a pause Said, "Yes, sir, and with all my heart." "Then let us send for a priest," said Robin Hood "And be married before we do part."

The following ballad in Child's volume, however, is called *Robin Hood and Maid Marian* in the table of contents but is also titled *A Famous Battle between Robin Hood and Maid Marian, Declaring Their Love, Life, and Liberty (Anonymous, 1700)*. This was where we saw earlier the description of our lady heroine as "a bonny fine maid of a noble degree." In this version, Robin Hood was referred to as Lord of Huntington and seemed to have been in love with Maid Marian for some long while:

V. 4	The Earl of Huntington, nobly born, That came of noble blood, To Marian went, with a good intent, By the name of Robin Hood.
V. 5	With kisses sweet their red lips meet, For shee and the earl did agree; In every place, they kindly imbrace, With love and sweet unity.

After they parted, Maid Marian returned to her home, while Robin Hood went into the greenwood. Yet, his lady love was restless with worry about him and pined away so much that she disguised herself as a page and went into the forest to find him. Robin Hood, also in disguise, came upon her but did not recognize her and she did not recognize him either.

This resulted in their both drawing their swords and getting into a fight that lasted "an hour or more" with each of them receiving a few wounds. The combat only ceased after Robin Hood paused and tried to convince his skilled foe to join his band of fighters in the greenwood.

V. 13
>When Marian did hear the voice of her love,
>Her self shee did quickly discover,
>And with kisses sweet she did him greet,
>Like to a most loyall lover.

V. 14
>When bold Robin Hood his Marian did see,
>Good lord, what clipping was there!
>With kind imbraces, and jobbing of faces,
>Providing of gallant cheer.

Robin Hood then took her to his camp for a great feast and everyone welcomed her and gave her a toast. This is very similar to the account in Chapter Seven of Green's book *The Adventures of Robin Hood*, because Green drew on the old ballads for his work.

Even though Maid Marian was only occasionally mentioned in the ballads, she was a memorable figure, which is why she was almost always included as a character in the interpretations that followed. Those will be referred to later but now it is time to examine the traits that have influenced the way most people see her.

The Different Faces of Maid Marian

In the early tales, Maid Marian was a versatile character, and as time went on, she became more complex. As she was weaved into story after story, she took on different characteristics. Of course, she was a romantic interest and, like a lot of female characters in Western tradition, a damsel in distress. But she was also much more.

Roger Lancelyn Green depicted Maid Marian as a noblewoman and a brave and skilled fighter. She could deftly handle a bow and arrow as well as she could a sword, even being Robin Hood's equal with both weapons. This part of her character did not just appear with Green's work, though. Remember, his story was a culmination of all the earlier ballads and literary references. Skill and strength have long been among Marian's major traits, but this never made her seem manly. Rather, she became a type of huntress figure, like the goddess Artemis of Greek mythology.

In Green's and many other adaptations of the legend, Maid Marian dressed in men's clothing when she joined Robin Hood and the foresters in Sherwood. Even so, she was never stripped of her femininity. Just as important as her courage and swordsmanship was her virginal purity and her nurturing spirit.

She was often portrayed as caring a great deal about everyone—not just Robin Hood. This capacity for compassion and kindness was another reason why Robin fell in love with her. She was always described as beautiful, and this was what initially attracted Robin to her. However, she was also surprisingly fleshed out more than the other beautiful female characters in the English literature from the medieval period well into the 19th century—most of which was written by men.

Another role she took, which we will especially see in our examination of the films in which she featured, was that of an informant or spy. Sometimes she was described as the cousin of King Richard or Prince John, and in other iterations, she was a ward of the monarchs, being the daughter of a lord. Since Robin Hood had been gentrified in the 16th century, there were many depictions of Marian as his childhood friend or acquaintance.

In any case, with this noble stature, she was privy to information to which commoners would not have had access. No doubt, this made her someone very convenient to include in tales about the outlaw, who was forced from aristocratic society.

Speaking of society, it is probably not surprising that Maid Marian changed with the times. Her agency waxed or waned, depending on the era in which she was being presented. Sometimes she was more passive while at others, her intelligence, dexterity, and courage were central to the plot moving forward. For instance, the Victorians had her relegated to a far more two-dimensional maiden than most of her depictions—both before and after their time. In contrast, late 20th century novels and other forms of media made Maid Marian an adventurer again.

Also dependent upon the period of history was how quickly she warmed to the man whom she loved. Several historians have felt that her exclusion from the earlier ballads of Robin Hood was because he was very antagonistic toward both the rules of religion and society. Any woman, least of all the chaste, highborn Lady Marian, could not have been seen with such a traitor.

Yet as attitudes evolved, so did her character. Throughout time she has been more than just the third person in a tense love triangle, or a means for Robin Hood to show off more of his skills. Could it be that a real person served as the inspiration for her character because of all the complex features she possessed—many more than most fictional characters overall?

As Oxford-educated author Marcus Pitcaithly remarks in his article "Matter of the Greenwood: Maid Marian - Origins" (Pitcaithly, 2013), the lady of legend whom we are studying is "even more shadowy than Robin himself."

It is futile to search for hard evidence of her being based on a woman who really lived, although that has not stopped people from trying. At best, it can be said that the evolution of Maid Marian may have been influenced by people in history, or even that parts of their stories were tacked onto hers.

Chapter Five

Lady Matilda Fitzwalter, born in the late 12th century, is believed by many to be the woman who inspired the fictional character who came to be known as Maid Marian. She was the daughter of Robert Fitzwalter, a wealthy lord and the feudal baron of Little Dunmow, Essex. The French historian Francisque Xavier Michel even dubbed him "one of the greatest men in England and one of the most powerful" (Wikipedia, 2023q).

The history of this famous man provides the foundation for the legend that would materialize around his daughter and also gives some context to the events going on at the time when Matilda lived (Alchetron, 2022).

The Tale of Robert, Baron Fitzwalter

Besides being a baron, Fitzwalter was also a knight banneret for the City of London and castellan of Castle Baynard. A castellan was a governor of a castle and its surrounding territory in the Middle Ages. Baron Fitzwalter originally served King John in the wars in Normandy—even being taken prisoner and forced to pay a heavy ransom for his freedom—but eventually, he grew resentful of the misgovernment of the king, so he began to gather a group of other barons to build opposition to King John. It was likely that financial reasons were one of the primary instigators in the conspiracy of 1212, but a situation with Lady Matilda was also cited.

Baron Fitzwalter claimed that King John made passes at his eldest daughter during a banquet and other barons also made similar comments. Whether or not this was a major contributing factor to what came next will never be known, but a romanticized legend sprang up around this event.

The pope of the time, Pope Innocent III, granted the barons an absolution from their allegiance to King John, who grew paranoid that the barons would try and capture him. When King John ordered each of them to send a relative to him as a hostage, Baron Fitzwalter refused and was exiled. He fled to France. In retaliation, the king destroyed Castle Baynard and seized Baron Fitzwalter's other estates.

A few months later, though, King John submitted to the pope and as part of the reconciliation, he restored Baron Fitzwalter's lands and allowed him to come back to England. But it seemed that the damage had already been done.

Robert, Baron Fitzwalter, continued to lead a baronial revolt against the king. By 1215, the barons had withdrawn their loyalty to King John once again, even threatening to wage war against him if he did not agree to their demands. When he hesitated, they began to build up their arms and named Baron Fitzwalter as their general, where he would preside over the "army of God."

Finally, the barons were able to force King John to sign the Magna Carta, which was a charter of rights that limited the king's power. In simple terms, it said that the king was not above the law. One clause stipulated that exile could not be enforced without a fair and lawful trial, which was probably one of Baron Fitzwalter's additions because he had been exiled from England previously.

Even with this, peace did not come between the barons and their king. Only a few months after the signing of the Magna Carta, war broke out between them. During the battles, Baron Fitzwalter attempted to convince people to accept Louis of France as their foreign king (France and England had long been rivals by this point), but he was ultimately unsuccessful.

When King John died in October 1216, the people accepted his heir, Henry III, as their new king. Even the French lost respect for the barons, especially Fitzwalter, because they had gone against their own lord and were, ultimately, traitors. Yet Baron Fitzwalter continued his allegiance with France.

In the Second Battle of Lincoln in 1217, the barons were defeated, and Baron Fitzwalter was taken prisoner, as was his son, Robert. He was released five months later, joined the Crusades the following year, and was reinstated to the aristocracy under Henry III. The charter he had helped put together and forced King John to sign was also reissued, and Baron Fitzwalter lived in peace during his later years until his death in 1235.

Since then, a legendary legacy was conjured around him as being a champion of England's liberty, especially in his homeland of Dunmow. On a much more global scale, however, is the story that grew around his daughter.

The Legend of Lady Matilda Fitzwalter

It was 1212 when Baron Fitzwalter's opposition to King John really came to a head. As with many historical events of this period, the details are unknown and there have been several different versions of what happened.

For instance, one says that Prince John (still only a prince since his brother, King Richard, was away fighting in the Crusades) hosted a feast and games. But another says it was Baron Fitzwalter himself who supposedly held a grand banquet. This included a tournament for knights, and many noble guests were invited. Regardless, it seems that the beautiful and charming eighteen-year-old Lady Matilda was in attendance.

Prince John appeared to be smitten by her, wishing to take her as his mistress. He made advances to her, but she snubbed them all. By most accounts, the prince was a repugnant and self-serving man. It is also highly possible that Lady Matilda shared her father's animosity towards him.

The legend states that on the fourth day of the festivities, an unfamiliar knight entered the tournament. He was extraordinarily skilled and swiftly vanquished all the others in the games. They were no competition for his talents and agility. Lady Matilda, who had become the "queen" of the banquet, marveled at his prowess and it was she who awarded the singular knight with a golden collar. Afterwards, he disappeared into the forest, before anyone could determine his identity.

At this point, the different versions clash again. We know from history that Baron Fitzwalter was exiled at this time. The romanticized tale claims it was because Prince John was furious that both Lady Matilda and her father rejected him. Legend also purports that he was so angry, he had Baron Fitzwalter slain during a siege upon his castle, causing Lady Matilda to flee her home.

Where did she go? Into the forest, of course, following the footsteps of the knight who had stolen her heart during the tournament. And she found him, no longer donning armor, but a verdant green archer's outfit, as were the others who lived in the forest with him.

It was revealed that the mysterious man was none other than the former Earl of Huntingdon, now become an outlaw who led his merry men in ploys to plague Prince John and his cronies. Yes, it was Robin Hood, who took it upon himself to protect Lady Matilda, together with her honor, from the vile and lusty prince.

The story tells how Lady Matilda changed her name to Marian (sometimes spelled Marion) and began to dress in male clothing to disguise herself. However, despite this, Prince John discovered her whereabouts and ordered an attack against the foresters.

Apparently, during the battle that ensued, Prince John confronted Lady Matilda himself. She did not cower from him but put up quite a defence—so much so that the prince withdrew in shame. Lady Matilda—as Marian—wed Robin soon afterwards.

Chapter five

Some time passed and King Richard returned to the land and restored Robin's earldom, thus making Lady Matilda the Countess of Huntingdon. But Robin and his lady only had a short time to enjoy their status as a noble couple, for when King Richard passed away, the crown passed to Prince John. As king, John held much more power.

One of King John's first tasks? To outlaw Robin, Earl of Huntingdon, once again. So, Lady Matilda fled with Robin into the forest, where they lived as they had before. But only a few years later, the outlaw hero died, and the common folk of the land mourned his loss greatly, as did Lady Matilda. Now in danger of King John's maliciousness, she sought refuge in a nunnery (Atlas Obscura, 2020).

Thus, she came to the Dunmow Priory, which her baronial family had patronized. There, she thought she was safe from the king, but she was, unfortunately, wrong, for it seemed that King John could hold quite a grudge.

Pretending to broker peace with her, he sent a chivalrous knight named Robert de Medewe to Dunmow Priory with a gift for her, and Sir Robert was allowed to see her because of his fine reputation. Poor de Medewe was instantly enamored with Lady Matilda, and completely oblivious that he had brought about her demise. He thought the gift he bestowed on her was only a bracelet—a token of reconciliation and King John's goodwill. Alas, the bracelet was poisoned.

Shortly after the knight left, Matilda put the bracelet around her wrist. Meanwhile, de Medewe could not shake his growing passion for the woman who was no longer young but still very beautiful. He turned around and headed back to Dunmow Priory, but as he neared the building, he heard a funeral dirge.

According to the legend, Lady Matilda had turned deathly pale as the bracelet burned through her wrist right to the bone. She had perished within moments. When Robert de Medewe came upon her corpse, which had been laid out on a bed of flowers, he flung himself on top of her in grief. He had been completely unaware of his part in King John's dastardly plan, and his sorrow at learning what he had done was great.

In fact, de Medewe refused to return to court and even gave up his knighthood. He became an Augustine monk thereafter. As for Lady Matilda, she was immortalized not just in this legend, but also in an alabaster sculpture that adorns her tomb, which sits in the Priory Church of Little Dunmow, St Mary the Virgin—one of the oldest buildings in Essex. The figure has been sculpted with a gracious smile, which it is said, Lady Matilda wore, even in death (Atlas Obscura, 2020).

Whether the real Lady Matilda Fitzwalter (also sometimes written as Fitzwater) went through these events, or the story was conjured up and attributed to her is unknown. Possibly, elements of each are true. The conundrum is at least partly due to the legend that was recorded in two plays written over four centuries ago by Anthony Munday (Britannica, 2007).

Chapter Six

Anthony Munday's Robin Hood Plays

In 1598, during the Elizabethan era, English dramatist, poet, and translator Anthony Munday, possibly assisted by Henry Chettle, penned two plays surrounding the legend of Robin Hood and his companions. Some consider both to be unfinished or, at the very least, unpolished. Nevertheless, they have endured.

Some of Munday's source material was inevitably *Matilda, the faire and chaste Daughter of the Lord Robert Fitzwater* by Michael Drayton which came out around 1594 (Drayton, 2010). The first of the plays was titled *The Downfall of Robert, Earle of Huntingdon, afterwards called Robin Hood, with his Love to Chaste Matilda, the Lord Fitzwater's daughter, afterwards his faire Maid Marian* in the edition where it originally saw print in 1601 (Reynolds's News and Miscellany, 2010).

From this alone, we can make two determinations. Munday's work is the first known text to connect Robin Hood with Robert, Earl of Huntingdon, which we will see had a tremendous influence on the characterization of him in just about everything that came after. In addition, he linked Lady Matilda Fitzwalter (Fitzwater in Munday's texts) forever to Maid Marian, which, inevitably, had the same effect.

This is somewhat confusing because in *The Downfall of Robert, Earle of Huntingdon*, Marian is called just that for the first part of the play, being identified as the daughter of Lord Lacy, but after line 781, is referred to as Matilda, the daughter of Lord Fitzwater. It seems she should have been Matilda at the beginning, because she changed her name to Marian when she joined Robin Hood and his band of outlaws and took on a new identity, as described earlier.

In any case, what is missing in most later renditions of the tale is the affection of Eleanor of Aquitaine, mother of King Richard and Prince John, for Robin Hood. This is one of the barriers to Robin and Marian's love, as is Prince John's desire for Lady Marian—which is more familiar. Strangely, though, Prince John is the utmost villain in this version—the aristocracy that causes "the downfall" of Robin Hood. Thus, it is more of a political tale than one about a legendary hero.

The work is a play within a play. At the start, two characters, Sir John Eltham and John Skelton describe the performance they are about to put on for the court of King Henry VIII. Eltham will be playing the part of Little John, while Skelton is to be Friar Tuck. The two of them discuss the play for a short time, with Skelton urging the audience to watch until the end.

Then we learn that Robin Hood has just been outlawed, thanks to his uncle, the Prior of York. As Earl of Huntingdon, (a title stripped from him when he was outlawed), Robin was served by a steward, Warman, who also plotted against him and eventually became the Sheriff of Nottingham. Lady Marian first entered the play at line 195, and you can clearly see the romantic drama building between her and Robin:

[Enter Marian.]

[line 195]
Marian   Why is my Lord so sad? Wherefore so soone,
So sodainely arose yee from the boorde?
Alas my Robin, what distempering griefe
Drinkes up the roseat colour of thy cheekes?
Why art thou silent? Answere mee my love.

[line 200]	
Robin	Let him, let him, let him make thee as sad.
	Hee hath a tongue can banish thee from joy,
	And chase thy crimson colour from thy cheekes
	Why speakest thou not? I pray thee Little John,
	Let the short story of my long distresse
	Be uttered in a word. What mean'st thou to protract?
	Wilt thou not speake? Then Marian list to mee.
	This day thou wert a maide, and now a spowse,
	Anone (poore soule) a widdowe thou must bee:
	Thy Robin is an outlawe, Marian,
	His goods and landes must be extended on,
	Himselfe exilde from thee, thou kept from him,
	[She sinkes in his armes.]
	By the long distance of unnumbred miles.
[line 215]	Faint'st thou at this? Speake to mee Marian,
	My olde love newely met, parte not so soone;
	Wee have a little time to tarry yet.
Marian	If but a little time, let mee not stay,
	Part wee today, then will I dye today.

Prompted by Little John, Robin comforted Marian, then told her to go and get the Queen, whom he suspected may have had something to do with his being outlawed (though he mostly called out his uncle and steward). The Queen was disgruntled by his suspicions and after Robin left, she told Marian:

[line 380]	
Queene	I can and will forget deserving hate,
	And give him comfort in this wofull state.
	Marian, I knowe Earle Roberts whole desire
	Is to have thee with him from hence away;
	And though I loved him dearely to this day,
	Yet since I see hee dearlier loveth thee,
	Thou shalt have all the furtherance I may.

The Queen then made a plan, telling Lady Marian that the two of them would swap their clothes, presumably so that Marian would be safe. But our intelligent heroine suspected that there was a plot afoot:

[line 415]

Marian I thanke your Highnesse, [*Aside*] but I will not trust ye,
My Robert shall have knowledge of this shift:
For I conceive alreadie your deepe drift.

Marian was right, of course. The Queen expected that Robin would whisk her away, thinking that she was his lady love. Then, she would have motive to denounce him as a traitor and a kidnapper, because she was jealous of his feelings for Marian.

The Queen's plot was foiled and shortly afterward, at line 790, Marian was listed as Matilda when she was on stage. Even after Robin changed his own name to Robin Hood and declared that Matilda would be his Maid Marian, she was still called Matilda—sometimes. Every so often, her name returned to Marian, such as in these consecutive lines when she gathered with the merry men:

Matilda Matilda is as joyfull of thy good,
As joy can make her. How fares Robin Hood?

Robin Well, my Matilda, and if thou agree,
Nothing but mirth shall waite on thee and mee.

Marian O God, how full of perfect mirth were I,
To see thy griefe turnd to true jollitie!

As you can see, the mixing up of names certainly seems to lend itself to the idea that Lady Matilda Fitzwater was at least the basis for the character for Marian. A few lines later, Little John, chivalrously giving Lady Marian a say in the matter, declared:

Chapter Six

Little John	Next tis agreed (if thereto shee agree)
	That faire Matilda henceforth change her name,
	And while it is the chance of Robin Hoode,
	To live in Sherewodde a poore outlawes life,
	She, by Maid Marians name, be only cald.

The love between Lady Marian and Robin Hood is also clear from this play. Written in such an early time, it is very nice to see that it is a more equal partnership than others of the period.

Marian	Marian hath all, sweete Robert, having thee,
	And guesses thee as rich, in having mee.
Robin	I am indeede,
	For having thee, what comfort can I neede?

Then, when Robin Hood was talking to Lord Fitzwater who was upset that Lady Marian had changed her name from Matilda, he declared his honorable intentions toward her and Lord Fitzwater was content that their love was pure.

Robin	Why? Shee is cald Maid Marian, honest friend,
	Because she lives a spotlesse maiden life,
	And shall, till Robins outlawe life have ende,
	That he may lawfully take her to wife;
	Which, if King Richard come, will not be long;
	For, in his hand is power to right our wrong.
Fitzwater	If it be thus, I joy in her names change.
	So pure love in these times is very strange.

After some more side plots were uncovered, King Richard returned from the Crusades. Then, Robin revealed Maid Marian's true identity as Matilda Fitzwater and asked for her hand, which King Richard granted.

Scene xv [line 2765]

Robin   This last I give, as tenants do their lands,
With a surrender, to receive againe,
The same into their owne possession:
No Marian, but Fitzwaters chast Matilda,
The precious jewell that poore Huntington
Doth in this world hold as his best esteeme.
Although with one hand I surrender her,
I holde the other, as one looking still,
Richard returnes her: so I hope he will.

King   Els God forbid. Receive thy Marian backe,
And never may your love be separate,
But florish fairely to the utmost date.

Since the Elizabethan period would have deemed sword fights and a lot of action a little too vulgar, *The Downfall of Robert* is quite static. It focuses largely on the intrigues at court and monologues of the main characters. The sequel is more of a tragedy and Lady Matilda takes center stage with Robin having only a small part even though the title still bears his name.

The Death of Robert, Earl of Huntingdon

When the two plays are staged together, Munday's second play about the greenwood mythology is frequently regarded as part two. It also had a long title upon its printing: *The Death of Robert, Earle of Huntingdon, otherwise called Robin Hood of Merry Sherwood, with the lamentable Tragedy of chaste Matilda, his fair maid Marian, poisoned at Dunmow by King John* (Munday & Chettle, 1601). This one began in a similar way to *The Downfall* and listed the character of our heroine as Matilda, Robin Hood's Maid Marian. As in the other play, sometimes the character names changed, seemingly for no reason.

Following a tradition of double plays, Munday made the first one lean more in the direction of comedy, while *The Death*, tends to the tragic. In this play, the Prior of York and Sir Doncaster decided to poison Robin Hood. They made an eerie prediction as they watched Marian happily strewing flower petals about (Munday, 1601).

Chapter Six

[Line 484]

Doncaster   How busy mistress Marian is?
　　　　　　　She thinkes this is her day of bliss.

Prior　　　But it shall be the woeful'st day
　　　　　　　That ever chanc'd her, if I may.

Soon afterward, Robin drank the poison and fell ill. His dying was long and drawn out, as he gave a few speeches and laid his head in Marian's lap (who was now called Matilda). Just before he took his last breath, Matilda lamented:

[Line 795]

Matilda　　O let me looke forever in thy eyes,
　　　　　　　And lay my warme breath to thy bloodlesse lips,
　　　　　　　If my sight can restraine death's tyrannies,
　　　　　　　Or keepe lives breath within thy bosome lock't.

Robin Hood's passing marked the end of Act I and the next four acts put Matilda in the spotlight. Further examples of the text will not be discussed here, since it can be laborious to read and there are many other literary works to consider. Just know that she was pursued relentlessly by King John throughout. Her uncle, Lord Bruce, tried to stand up to him, and his wife and youngest son were imprisoned in a dungeon where they suffered starvation. Eventually, Matilda fled to Dunmow Abbey for shelter. King John sent one of his men to poison her there. Only then did the wicked king repent his actions.

It must be clear by now just how much the story—whether real or exaggerated—of the real Lady Matilda Fitzwalter impacted Munday's works. And in turn, his plays affected the legend of Robin Hood and Maid Marian forever.

The Tragedy of King John and Matilda by Robert Davenport (Davenport, 2011), written in the mid-1600s, borrowed quite a lot from Munday's *The Death of Robert, Earle of Huntingdon*. At the start, King John and his cronies had tense dealings with the barons who had forced the king to sign the Magna Carta. The king also lustfully pursued Matilda, one of the baron's daughters, and when the queen came upon her, she called Matilda a harlot and scratched her.

In this tale, Matilda was rescued by Lord Bruce, whose family was then thrown into prison and starved. Matilda was captured twice more, and by then, the queen had warmed to her charm and helped her take refuge in an abbey. Even after King John promised to divorce his wife and make Matilda queen, she refused him, remaining chaste and pure. The rejected monarch decided that if she would not have him, she must die.

He sent a messenger to the abbey with a poisoned glove. Matilda was killed by the "gift" yet remained a paragon of virtue. Finally remorseful, King John reconciled with the barons, as well as with his wife, and the last scene depicted Matilda's funeral.

Before we move on to our next section, there is one more hypothesis that is critical to mention. There has been some doubt that Lady Matilda Fitzwalter had such a big influence on the character of Maid Marian. Some people think she may have been confused with another woman entirely, who was the true real-life counterpart of our heroine.

The name Maud 'Matilda' Vavasour, a woman of the early 1200s, has come up in discussions of this nature, especially because it was reputed that she had been desired by the King (*Wikipedia*, 2021). Her origins are a little complex, but she may also have been known as Matilda Walter after her first marriage. Yet it is her second marriage to one Fouke FitzWarin (with name variants of Fulk, FitzWaryn, or Fouke le Fitz Waryn) that provides the most evidence for her link to Maid Marian.

Fouke FitzWarin is one of many possibilities for Robin Hood being based on a real-life man. He was one of King John's enemies who was outlawed for three years and later rebelled against the monarch for a second time.

A lengthy romance, written as early as 1260, seems to cite him as the principal character, and this romance shares a considerable number of similarities with *A Gest of Robyn Hode*, also known as *A Lytell Geste of Robyn Hode*, the minstrel ballad that had much influence on the legendary figure (Child, 1888a; Wikipedia, 2023f). And with this, it is time to take a quick diversion to learn more about Robin, since he is so important in Lady Marian's life.

Chapter Seven

About Robin Hood

We have talked a lot about Lady Marian so far, but it is also important to highlight the man she loved and whose wife she became in most of the variations on the legend. Though this is not his book, Robin is a central figure to Marian's story and evolution. So, an account of Robin is included. However, the account will be concise even though he becomes significantly more exciting when partnered with Marian.

The popular perception of Robin Hood is, of course, as an outlaw who robbed the rich and gave to the poor, with the help of his band of merry men. The phrase "merry men" originated in the Middle Ages as a general term for a group of men who were following an outlaw or a knight. The expression is most famously used to recount the exploits of Robin Hood's band of outlaws. Robin's merry men were first described in the ballad *Robin Hood and the Monk* (Wikipedia, 2024c)

Works that feature Robin place his setting anywhere between the 12th and 14th centuries. Most often, his tale was set in medieval England, when Richard the Lionheart was king but had left his country to fight in the Crusades. Usually, Robin Hood was a Saxon, who felt the oppression of the unjust Normans, of whom, Prince John—Richard's brother who was put in charge until the

Lionheart returned—was the worst. Sometimes, though, the green-clad archer was considered to be a rebellious Norman noble.

So, since there are some historical miscellanea in his tale, is it possible that Robin Hood could have been based on a real individual from history? The answer, just as it is with Marian, is *maybe*.

Often in Robin Hood stories, Robin was referred to as *Wolfshead*. This stems from the Latin phrase *caput gerat lupinum* which translates to "let him bear the head of a wolf." It was once used to define a criminal who had committed a heinous crime and was no longer protected by the law. Such a person was viewed as a pariah and was vulnerable to assault from anyone. To make someone an outlaw whose head was worth as much as a wolf's, whether it was dead or alive, the court would declare them *caput gerat lupinum*, or just *caput lupinum* (Anonymous, 2025).

There were outlaws, such as Fouke FitzWarin, mentioned in the previous chapter (together with variations of the name), who could have been something of an influence on the legend. One of the oldest surviving historical documents containing a Robin Hood was a court register from 1226 that listed him as a fugitive. A William Robehod was recorded in a similar fashion in 1262. And, in 1354, there was a document which discussed a prisoner awaiting trial who went by the name Robin Hood. It seems that the name was used by a variety of outlaws in different times and regions in England (Wikipedia, 2023ab).

Thus, most historians agree that Robin Hood as we have come to know him is mostly fictional. No matter, he is more familiar than many real people. In fact, there are very many places all over England that bear the legendary outlaw's name, including Robin Hood's Well in Barnsdale Forest, Yorkshire and Robin Hood's Bay, also in Yorkshire as well as Robin Hood's Cave and Robin Hood's Stoop in Derbyshire, to mention but a few (Dobson & Taylor, 1989a). However, since he is apparently a mythical invention, the books must be consulted.

We have already discussed his origins as a May Games character and a figure of French poetry so we will not dwell on those again. And though his stock traits have changed since then, they have not transformed anywhere near as much as those of Maid Marian. So, it is now appropriate to look briefly at the works about Robin Hood where Marian does not appear.

THE FIRST APPEARANCE OF ROBIN HOOD IN TEXT

The first time Robin was seen in a text was in *The Vision of William concerning Piers Plowman in Three Parallel Texts* by William Langland, where a drunken priest, Sloth, could not recite the Lord's Prayer perfectly but knew rhymes about Robin Hood and Randolf, the earl [*sic*] of Chester (Langland, c.1377). Little is known about the author, but the allegorical poem credited to him is dated to around 1377. It is highly lauded as a medieval work of literature that predates Geoffrey Chaucer's *Canterbury Tales* (Britannica, 2024b).

For our purposes here, there was only a passing reference to Robin Hood that suggested he might be popular among peasants and in tavern songs but was not really of much importance to those of higher classes. But he did not stay that way.

Stephen Knight's detailed book about Robin Hood tells us that there were many ballads about him—seven pre-1600 ones that have survived, and twenty-seven from the following century (Knight, 2000). We have looked at a few already, and now it is time to consider further some of the other prominent titles that did not always include Maid Marian.

One of the oldest ballads is *Robin Hood and the Monk* from the 15th century (Child, 1888c), set in Sherwood Forest and featuring the hero's big right-hand man, Little John. Though some later depictions of Little John portrayed him as a bumbling musclehead, this Little John was wise. He warned Robin Hood not to leave the forest, but the outlaw did not listen.

When Robin went into Nottingham for Mass, he was recognized by a monk who promptly set the sheriff on him. The monk headed to the castle to tell the king, but Little John, and another merry man named Much, murdered him, as well as his page, on the road. Then the foresters posed as the monk and his servant and told the news of Robin Hood's capture to the king, earning themselves a big reward. Once the tricky pair returned to Nottingham, they freed Robin Hood and went back to the forest.

While the murders of the monk and page may seem brutally violent to our modern sensibilities, people of the Middle Ages were, unfortunately, used to such happenings. Violence happened all too often. Public hangings were common, with bodies often left out in the open. However, unlike the story shown in *Robin Hood and the Monk* and many other ballads from the same era that have survived, it typically happened the other way around.

As J. Rubén Valdés Miyares wrote in an article for *National Geographic*, "these early Robin Hood ballads begin to show a turning of the tables, in which the lower classes are able to punish the upper classes through trickery and violence" (Valdés-Miyares, 2019).

One of the longest of the ballads of the 15th century was *A Gest of Robyn Hode* also known as *A Lyttell Gest of Robyn Hode* or *A Merry Gest of Robyn Hode* (Child, 1888a). This is one of the earliest examples describing the outlaw as stealing from wealthy aristocrats for the benefit of the underprivileged peasants (Wikipedia, 2023f). The author is unknown, but the work appears to be a compilation of many songs and poems about the figure, most of which are now lost. In this version, Robin Hood was a yeoman, or of the middle class. Yeomen were often servants of nobles, and here, Robin Hood was a yeoman of the king. But it was King Edward, not Richard, who was his liege.

A Gest tells how Robin Hood missed the forest, so he abandoned his post and became a medieval avenger. He gave Little John a list of people whom the merry men were allowed to rob or murder. The list included the Sheriff of Nottingham, as well as some bishops, archbishops, and villainous nobles. Peasants and yeomen were not to be harmed.

The ballad turned rather bloody. At one point, Robin Hood sliced the throat of the sheriff after shooting him with his bow and arrow. Other texts of the period have just as much gore. In *Robin Hood and Guy of Gisborne*, Robin Hood killed his archnemesis and enjoyed mutilating the body (Child, 1888b).

By the time he entered the May Games, he was not as sadistic or violent but was more of a trickster figure. He also began to gain popularity among the nobility, the class in which he would become a member in Anthony Munday's interpretation. There was also a bit of royal gossip, that told of lusty King Henry VIII in 1510 dressing in a Robin Hood costume and ambushing his young queen, Catherine of Aragon, in her bedchamber. He danced and flitted about the room to entertain her and her ladies-in-waiting (Hall, 1809, p. 513). Oh, if only he had stayed such a fun-loving spouse!

MAID MARIAN AND FRIAR TUCK JOIN THE NARRATIVE

It was around this time in the 16th century that Maid Marian and Friar Tuck joined Robin Hood in some of the stories. Plays that were written for the aristocracy often began to feature him as a character. We have already read about Anthony Munday's, but even William Shakespeare used him in some of his plays. It was Munday, though, who transformed him into a noble, the Earl of Huntingdon, and thus, brought a whole new level of popularity to the legend.

Since then, so many authors have been inspired to reinvent Robin Hood. In 1820, Sir Walter Scott published *Ivanhoe*, which had Locksley as one of the characters. Locksley turned out to be Robin Hood, the "King of Outlaws". The book was republished by Penguin in 2000 (Scott, 2000). Taking a page from Munday, Scott portrayed the figure as an honorable Englishman who was loyal to King Richard.

Sixty years later, Howard Pyle both wrote and illustrated an edition of the story for children, first published in 1883. *The Merry Adventures of Robin Hood* became an instant hit and would become hugely influential to those who wanted to retell the tale in various forms later (Pyle, 2018). This, together with Francis James Child's anthology of popular ballads which collected so many of the older Robin Hood ditties, caused a surge of interest in the legend, particularly in the United States. Since then, the character and his adventures have been featured in many other children's books.

The previously mentioned novel, *The Adventures of Robin Hood* by Roger Lancelyn Green, was later added to the pile of great works about the outlaw. He credits many of the ballads, plays, and other texts we have brought up so far as inspiration for his classic, as well as some we will soon see in the next chapter.

Green's tale commenced with the birth of the boy who would become Robin Hood. His father, William Fitzooth, was turned away by Sir George Gamwell when he asked for Gamwell's daughter Joanna's hand in marriage. But the two married secretly anyway, and some months later, William spirited the pregnant Joanna away in the middle of the night to the forest. Robert Fitzooth was born in the very woods he would later make his lair. When Sir George found his daughter, he was overcome with affection for his new grandson and forgave William Fitzooth.

The next scene involved Much the Miller's Son, who was accused of killing a deer in the king's forest. Prince John interrogated Much about the outlaw of whom he had heard stories. Much claimed, "I know not who he is! Robin Hood comes out of the forest—men say he is the Good Spirit of Sherwood—and having brought help, he goes away as silently as he came. No one has seen him by daylight." This was how we were introduced to the outlaw who went on to have many adventures.

If anything, this short summary of the literary history of Robin Hood has shown just how important a figure he was and still is to Western culture, and indeed, all of humanity. Green was quite correct when he wrote, "Robin Hood's is a story that can never die, nor cease to fire the imagination. Like the old fairy tales it must be told and told again—for like them it is touched with enchantment and few of us can fail to come under its spell" (Green, 2016b).

Chapter Eight

Let us return now to the literature that brings Robin Hood and Maid Marian together. For when the two of them appear in any version of the legend, the story is all the richer for having them both in it, instead of just one or the other. You see, not only is Maid Marian Robin Hood's partner, but her function in the stories is also quite different from his—she is an essential complement to him. However, despite this fact, most of the 17th century works to feature Robin Hood exclude Maid Marian, except for a brief mention in *A True Tale of Robin Hood* by Martin Parker, first published in 1632 (Parker, 2018).

In the anonymously-authored 1819 novel *Robin Hood: A Tale of the Olden Times*, Marian did not make any appearance (Anonymous, 1819). Strangely, in this two-volume work, the love interest was named Claribel and this was probably a reference to *The Faerie Queene* by Edmund Spenser (Wikipedia, 2024b).

But around this time, there *was* a novella featuring Maid Marian. It was one of the earliest novels written about our heroine. Although it appeared in 1822, most of it was written four years prior and is no longer well-known although many later authors, including Roger Lancelyn Green, turned to this work for inspiration.

Thomas Love Peacock's Maid Marian

The text to which we are referring is *Maid Marian*, by Thomas Love Peacock, largely written in 1818 completed and published in 1822 and now republished as part of *The Gutenberg Project* (Peacock, 2008). Peacock was an English poet and writer who largely wrote satirical novels which criticized the philosophical opinions of the day. One of Peacock's friends was the poet Percy Bysshe Shelley, with whom he traded letters. In one of these, Peacock wrote that the summer of 1818 was not "very favourable to intellectual exertion" but he was struck by a fancy to write something quite unlike his usual fare when "rivers, castles, forests, abbeys, monks, maids, kings, and banditti were all dancing before me like a masked ball." At this time, Peacock was writing his romance *Maid Marian*, and had completed all but the last three chapters (Wikipedia, 2023ak).

Before he could complete the work, he was called to be an official of the East India Company and the novella was not finished and published until 1822. Alas, by then, many people took it to be an imitation of Sir Walter Scott's *Ivanhoe*, in which Maid Marian did not feature at all (Scott, 2000). However, Peacock had written most of his work before Scott wrote his.

Peacock gave us a willful and strong female character who was not afraid to challenge gender stereotypes. Although Maid Marian still exhibited all the qualities that made her the heroine she was, this version of her seemed more brazen than earlier ones. There was even speculation that Peacock had based his main character on Mary Shelley, a friend who was married to Percy Bysshe Shelley and who had written the novel *Frankenstein*, published in 1818. So, was Maid Marian of the novella based on Mary Shelley?

Chapter 1 of *Maid Marian* begins with: " 'The Abbot, in his alb arrayed,' stood at the altar in the abbey-chapel of Rubygill, with all his plump, glossy, rosy friars, in goodly lines disposed, to solemnise the nuptials of the beautiful Matilda Fitzwater, daughter of the Baron of Arlingford, with the noble Robert Fitz-Ooth, Earl of Locksley and Huntingdon" (Peacock, 2023a).

Chapter Eight

Matilda was Marian and Fitz-Ooth was Robin Hood. Everyone was ready for the ceremony to commence, but Robert Fitz-Ooth had not yet appeared. "Matilda feared that some evil had befallen her lover, but felt no diminution of her confidence in his honour and love." With some militaristic fanfare, he arrived for his wedding, which was then interrupted by Sir Ralph Montfaucon and a party of armed men, acting here "in the call of King Henry" and claiming that Fitz-Ooth had been outlawed. The king at the beginning of this tale was Henry II, but shortly after the Gamwell feast, he died and was succeeded by Richard Cœur de Lion.

After kissing Matilda, Robert Fitz-Ooth left her to her father's care, then began a sword fight. The following sentence perfectly sums up the world that Peacock was writing in and how it contrasted with the medieval setting of his story: "Some of the women screamed, but none of them fainted; for fainting was not so much the fashion in those days, when the ladies breakfasted on brawn and ale at sunrise, as in our more refined age of green tea and muffins at noon."

This was followed by a fracas in which the abbot attempted to exit the chapel "as fast as his bulk and his holy gowns could allow." All the monks were at his heels, and when he tripped and fell, they also tripped and "fell over him and each other, and lay a rolling chaos of animated rotundities, sprawling and bawling in unseemly disarray." Peacock indeed sprinkled some of his unique brand of humor throughout his tale.

After this, a skirmish ensued during which the Earl of Huntingdon escaped. Those of the friars and king's men who were unharmed retired to raid the larder of venison, pastries, and wine. During the repast, they questioned Sir Ralph Montfaucon, the leader of the soldiers, respecting the nature of the earl's offence:

"A complication of offences," replied Sir Ralph . . . he began with hunting the king's deer" and "followed it up by contempt of the king's mandates, and by armed resistance to his power, in defiance of all authority;" and "withheld payment of certain moneys to the abbot of Doncaster, in denial of all law; and has thus made himself the declared enemy of church and state."

"Truly," said Sir Ralph, "I am sorry for the damsel: she seems fond of this wild runagate."

"A mad girl, a mad girl," said the little friar.

"How a mad girl?" said brother Michael. "Has she not beauty, grace, wit, sense, discretion, dexterity, learning, and valour?"

"Learning!" exclaimed the little friar; "what has a woman to do with learning? And valour! Who ever heard a woman commended for valour? Meekness and mildness, and softness, and gentleness, and tenderness, and humility, and obedience to her husband, and faith in her confessor, and domesticity, or, as learned doctors call it, the faculty of stayathomeitiveness, and embroidery, and music, and pickling, and preserving, and the whole complex and multiplex detail of the noble science of dinner, as well in preparation for the table, as in arrangement over it, and in distribution around it to knights, and squires, and ghostly friars—these—are female virtues: but valour—why who ever heard—?"

Again, Peacock was poking fun at the gender roles of his own time, while also detailing how women might have been seen at the end of the 12th century. He wrote about brother Michael, though, as defending Matilda ferociously, calling her "gentle as a ring-dove, yet high-soaring as a falcon: humble below her deserving . . . the chief regulator of her household, the fairest pillar of her hall, and the sweetest blossom of her bower" as well as many more complimentary attributes.

Sir Ralph told him, "If the young lady be half what you describe, she must be a paragon," but then commented that brother Michael's commending her for valor amazed him. The little friar then stated that Matilda was skilled in fencing, drawing the long bow, and using the singlestick and quarterstaff at which brother Michael was quick to amend any thoughts otherwise by saying, "but with such womanly grace and temperate self-command as if those manly exercises belonged to her only, and were become for her sake feminine."

Sir Ralph was so impressed by brother Michael's description of Matilda, he decided to pay her a visit. Both friars accompanied him. On the way, brother

Chapter Eight

Michael continued to sing her praises: "She has certainly a high spirit; but it is the wing of the eagle, without his beak or his claw. She is as gentle as magnanimous; but it is the gentleness of the summer wind, which, however lightly it wave the tuft of the pine, carries with it the intimation of a power, that, if roused to its extremity, could make it bend to the dust."

"From the warmth of your panegyric . . .," said Sir Ralph, "I should almost suspect you were in love with the damsel."

"So I am," said the friar, "and I care not who knows it; but in all the way of honesty, master soldier. I am, as it were, her spiritual lover; and were she a damsel errant, I would be her ghostly esquire, her friar militant." Perhaps this was an indication of her May Games iteration of being connected so closely to the friar?

Upon meeting with Matilda's father, Lord Fitzwater, Sir Ralph surmised that his "half-married" daughter was likely distressed. Fitzwater scoffed at this and said, "Not a whit, sir. She is, as usual, in a most provoking imperturbability, and contradicts me so smilingly that it would enrage you to see her."

Sir Ralph said that he wanted to see her, but before anyone could be sent to fetch her from her room, she appeared. Peacock, betraying the influence of the Romantics, described her in detail:

"Matilda not dreaming of visitors, tripped into the apartment in a dress of forest green, with a small quiver by her side, and a bow and arrow in her hand. Her hair, black and glossy as the raven's wing, curled like wandering clusters of dark ripe grapes under the edge of her round bonnet; and a plume of black feathers fell back negligently above it, with an almost horizontal inclination, that seemed the habitual effect of rapid motion against the wind. Her black eyes sparkled like sunbeams on a river: a clear, deep, liquid radiance, the reflection of ethereal fire,—tempered, not subdued, in the medium of its living and gentle mirror."

She told her father she was going hunting, and he forbade it. Then, Matilda managed to devise all the methods she would use to escape the castle should her father try to keep her confined therein. When she began to sing, brother Michael joined in, infuriating Lord Fitzwater further, but also placating him at the same time. He finally gave in and remarked to Sir Ralph, who was now completely smitten with Matilda, that although she was his daughter, she had him "in leading-strings."

Not long afterward, Sir Ralph attended the May Games where Matilda was crowned Queen of the May. Though he joined in the archery contest, each one of the foresters bettered him and he jealousy watched Matilda as she presented the winner with a golden arrow and then went to be his partner in the dance until the end of the feast. Sir Ralph was fully aware that this was the outlaw whom King Henry had commissioned him to apprehend. He asked William Gamwell, whose family was hosting the games, what might happen if he attempted to take him prisoner. Gamwell told Sir Ralph that he would be in grave danger from the company there gathered, and he should leave without delay.

Sir Ralph and his squire rode speedily to Nottingham and engaged the help of the sheriff and his men. They then were on their way back to the Gamwell feast but came upon a bridge where they met Matilda, Robert, the friar, and a handful of foresters blocking it. The sheriff and his men were quickly apprehended, with Matilda lodging an arrow in Sir Ralph's arm. Then, she approached the knight, swiftly removed her arrow, and bandaged the wound with her scarf, saying:

"I reclaim my arrow, sir knight, which struck where I aimed it, to admonish you to desist from your enterprise. I could as easily have lodged it in your heart."

"It did not need," said the knight, with rueful gallantry; "you have lodged one there already."

"If you mean to say that you love me," said Matilda, "it is more than I ever shall you: but if you will show your love by no further interfering with mine, you will at least merit my gratitude." Sir Ralph, probably a little put out, did not respond.

Since Matilda was always honest with her father about where she was going, he felt that her word was "a better security than locks and bars." That is, until a large group of unarmed men came to his castle and ordered him to lower the drawbridge. When Fitzwater asked them why, they told him that the sheriff was "bruised," Sir Ralph and many others were wounded, and his daughter, together with the friar and William Gamwell, were to be apprehended for their part in the affair.

Lord Fitzwater scoffed at this and sent the men on their way. However, he then interrogated Matilda, who told him all that had happened. Her father forbade her, much more seriously, to leave the castle grounds. Shortly afterward, they discovered that Gamwell had been caught and was to be hanged. Fortunately, the foresters saved him, and he then promptly changed his name to Will Scarlett.

But Matilda's health began to decline as she worried about her lover and her friends, especially as she was isolated from Robin Hood and the men of Sherwood Forest. Whilst conducting business in Nottingham, Prince John would ride past the castle of Arlingford. On one occasion, he decided to visit and partake of Lord Fitzwater's hospitality. He met and was immediately "grievously smitten by the charms of the lovely Matilda." A little later, he sent his traveling minstrel to "make proposals to the lady" thinking that his royal status would be enough to gain her affection. However, Matilda rejected his advances outright and Prince John was so angry at this "flagrant outrage on royal prerogative" that he promised to be revenged and determined "to obtain possession of the lady by force of arms" (Peacock, 2023b).

He assembled his men and marched on Fitzwater castle, but Lord Fitzwater and Matilda received a message delivered by a blunt arrow that flew through a window. Thus, they had time to secure the building while Prince John's men were constructing a wheeled machine which could be taken to the edge of the moat and used as a temporary bridge.

But in the middle of the night, Prince John woke to find that the machine was engulfed in flames. When he approached, he saw a forester fighting his warriors and by the side of this forester was none other than the fair Matilda. The prince asked her to yield, but she refused and even challenged him to fight with her. Her friend, brother Michael, who was now taking the name of Friar Tuck, laid the prince flat and his men had to carry him back to the tent while the foresters, together with Matilda and her father, escaped into Sherwood Forest.

There, the baron Fitzwater was introduced to the group that followed Robin Hood, his outlawed almost-son-in-law. Then he watched in dismay as Matilda was declared the queen of the forest. But Friar Tuck stepped in first.

"Not Matilda," he said. "The rules of our holy alliance require new birth. I sprinkle, not thy forehead with water, but thy lips with wine, and baptize thee Marian." Fitzwater was furious and thought that his daughter had renounced her name and parentage, but the former Matilda dismissed his worrying:

"I will always be your true daughter: I will always love, and serve, and watch, and defend you: but neither will I forsake my plighted love, and my own liege lord, who was your choice before he was mine, for you made him my associate in infancy; and that he continued to be mine when he ceased to be yours, does not in any way show remissness in my duties or falling off in my affections. And though I here plight my troth at the altar to Robin, in the presence of this holy priest and pious clerk, yet—Father, when Richard returns from Palestine, he will restore you to your barony, and perhaps, for your sake, your daughter's husband to the earldom of Huntingdon: should that never be, should it be the will of fate that we must live and die in the greenwood, I will live and die MAID MARIAN."

Robin heartily agreed that chastity be upheld, for he would never risk "the perils of maternity" when there were so many other dangers that they were facing in the moment. The baron was appeased, and the foresters rejoiced and sang the praises of their leaders, with these lyrics about our heroine:

Chapter Eight

> And what eye hath e'er seen such a sweet Maiden Queen,
> As Marian, the pride of the forester's green?
> A sweet garden-flower, she blooms in the bower,
> Where alone to this hour the wild rose has been:
> We hail her in duty the queen of all beauty:
> We will live, we will die, by our sweet Maiden queen *[sic]*.

When the feasting was done, Robin and Marian escorted Lord Fitzwater to the Gamwell estate, where he would be safe until King Richard's return. Although they disguised themselves as pilgrims coming back from Palestine, they happened upon Sir Ralph, who recognized the eyes of the woman in the party. "Those eyes, he thought, were certainly the eyes of Matilda Fitzwater; and if the eyes were hers, it was extremely probable, if not logically consecutive, that the rest of the body they belonged to was hers also."

Sir Ralph let them go on their way but attempted to ambush the small group after they stopped at a cottage for the night. Robin and Marian were prepared, and together with the help of Lord Fitzwater and the owners of the cottage, made swift work of the intruders. One last time, Marian warned Sir Ralph to leave her alone and to stop harassing the man she loved. Sir Ralph had no choice but to obey.

After depositing Marian's father at Gamwell, they returned to Sherwood. There, "Robin and Marian dwelt and reigned in the forest, ranging the glades and the greenwoods from the matins of the lark to the vespers of the nightingale, and administering natural justice according to Robin's ideas of rectifying the inequalities of human condition."

Much time passed this way until Marian, disguised as a man, came upon a "lusty broad boned knight" in the forest and engaged him in swordplay. They were quite the equals in fighting, and only halted the combat when Friar Tuck found them and begged them to stop. The knight was surprised when Marian disclosed that she was a woman, and he allowed her to lead him to Robin Hood's camp, where he dined with the band of foresters and listened to how devoted they were to Robin, Marian, and most of all, the true king, Richard the Lionheart (Peacock, 2023c).

At that point, the knight revealed himself as this very man. The foresters all fell to their knees, and King Richard told them that he was pleased with how Robin had fought against the corruption that had been taking place in his absence. He restored Robin's earldom, as well as the Fitzwater lands, and pardoned all the foresters.

Thereafter, Robin and Marian lived as "the earl and countess of Huntingdon, who led a discreet and courtly life, and kept up old hospitality in all its munificence, till the death of King Richard and the usurpation of John, by placing their enemy in power, compelled them to return to their greenwood sovereignty." Their followers joined them in the forest once again, and "in merry Sherwood they long lived together, the lady still retaining her former name of Maid Marian, though the appellation was then as much a misnomer as that of Little John."

This delightful tale of Peacock's, though not as critically acclaimed as Sir Walter Scott's *Ivanhoe* which came out around the same time, characterized Lady Marian in a way that had not been seen before. She was depicted more as an active character who made her own decisions and could defend herself with her excellent fighting skills. She defied social expectations, revealing her independence and power. She was no longer a damsel in distress but a key character in her own right.

Though *Maid Marian* was originally meant to be a satire on the renewed interest in medieval times that occurred in 1800s England when the government was looking back at strict monarchies, the impact it had on our heroine was undeniable, both far into the future, and during the century in which it appeared.

Chapter Nine

More Maid Marian texts of the 19th Century

Just thirty years after Peacock published his novella, Pierce Egan the Younger (Wikipedia, 2023o) and Joaquim Stocqueler (Wikipedia, 2023g) continued the tradition of the brave, feisty woman. Egan wrote a novel entitled *Robin Hood and Little John* which was initially serialized in 1838 and published in book form in 1840 (Egan, 2010). Stocqueler's *Maid Marian, the Forest Queen: A companion to Robin Hood* was intended to be a sequel to this (Stocqueler, 2010).

Serials were quite popular in Victorian times. And in many of these, Lady Marian was represented very differently from the female characters in other stories. Stephen Basdeo goes as far as calling her an "emancipated proto-feminist" in his paper read at the Women in Print Conference, Chetham's Library, Manchester on 20 May 2016 (Basdeo, 2016). Despite this fact, she was not adapted into any works by Victorian female authors, though they were being published and read more often than ever before. Yet many men were including Lady Marian in their tales, giving her greater autonomy than almost any other female character in fiction at the time.

Pierce Egan, in his highly successful Robin Hood novel, depicts her as strong, wise, and devoted to the democratic values upheld by the group in Sherwood Forest. She even asked to be called Marian, rather than her birth name of Matilda, so that no one would think she was above their station. Not only that, but she could match most men with a bow and arrow. In contrast, Egan's other women fainted regularly and were afraid to leave their homes.

Stocqueler raised the bar by making Lady Marian the central figure in the first section of his story. She was put in charge of the Sherwood Forest gang while Robin Hood joined King Richard in the Crusades. Again, in this narrative, Marian was a highly skilled archer, who regularly went hunting and even tussled with a wild boar in one scene. Yet Stocqueler was careful to emphasize that she was still very feminine and gentle. He even encouraged women readers to strive to be as independent and active as she was.

Even so, patriarchal authority was still the dominant way of society. And when Robin Hood returned in Stocqueler's version, Lady Marian was relegated to a weaker role. That is, until she was enchanted by a witch and almost poisoned everyone in Sherwood! Was this perhaps a subtle and completely unnecessary warning about women getting *too* much independence? Maybe, because many of the works that followed limited Lady Marian's self-determination again.

In 1865, an anonymous author wrote a serialized novel called *Little John and Will Scarlet or The Outlaws of Sherwood Forest* (Reynolds's News and Miscellany, 2016). By featuring two skilled women, Marian and Eveline, who saved the men from fatal danger, he proved his theory that "women are our best and safest shield from danger." The band of merry men needed their contributions.

But just four years later in 1869 (and republished in 2005), George Emmett published his novel of three volumes, *Robin Hood and the Outlaws of Sherwood Forest* and tore down what so many other previous writers had built (Emmett, 2005). Emmett's Marian was much more typical of the "damsel in distress" stereotype. She was regularly captured and had to wait for Robin to save her, having no sense of fortitude and indeed, no real sense at all. Marian even admitted as much in one scene, where she claimed, "I know but little, my tongue is guided by my heart."

This work was reprinted in 1885 as a penny dreadful (Wikipedia, 2023n). These were serials produced in the United Kingdom during the 19th century. They were published in weekly parts of eight to sixteen pages, at a cost of one penny each and many were specifically geared toward young men and boys. Unfortunately, Emmett's work stripped Maid Marian of her independence and individuality in these stories meant for the male youth of the time. So, those tales that could have influenced these young men by presenting the heroine, Maid Marian, as a strong, three-dimensional character, failed in that respect.

Alexandre Dumas, the famous author of *The Three Musketeers* and *The Count of Monte Cristo*, also tried his hand at the legend. He produced two books about Robin Hood which were published posthumously, and which possibly were based on Pierce Egan's work. Dumas' tales were entitled *The Prince of Thieves (Le Prince des voleurs)* first published in 1872 and the sequel *Robin Hood the Outlaw (Robin Hood le proscrit)* first published in 1873 and republished in 2021 (Dumas, 2021).

The first book, *The Prince of Thieves*, recounted Robin Hood's origin and youth, including his first encounters with the other familiar characters like Little John, Friar Tuck, and of course, Maid Marian. The follow-up, *Robin Hood the Outlaw*, continued the romance between Robin Hood and Maid Marian but had much less action. In addition, it also discussed many of the love lives of the merry men. Thus, in the second book, there were more female characters than in the majority of other texts inspired by the legend. Of course, we know Dumas was a skilled storyteller, and there is much to admire in his works on the legend.

Apart from these examples, our heroine largely remained a background figure in many retellings, especially as the Robin Hood stories were relegated to children's literature. Aldine's penny novels, collected as the *Robin Hood Library*, graced the market at the start of the 20th century (Aldine Robin Hood Library, 1901-1906). Maid Marian was hardly featured, and when she was mentioned, it was usually to spur Robin Hood to come and rescue her from the Sheriff of Nottingham or Prince John.

Alfred Lord Tennyson also wrote an interpretation of the story. His version was a play called *The Foresters* or *Robin Hood and Maid Marian* (Wikipedia, 2022). A set of incidental music to accompany the play was composed by Sir Arthur Sullivan. The play opened in New York in 1892 and went on to play in seven other American cities. There was a single performance of the play in London on the same night that it opened in New York, in order to secure the British copyright. An English production opened in London in 1893 but was not well received.

Almost at the beginning of the play there was commentary about gender roles (Alfred Lord Tennyson, n.d.). In the first scene, Little John entered the garden of Sir Richard of Lea's castle, musing to himself:

> "My master, Robin the Earl, is always a-telling us that every man, for the sake of the great blessed Mother in heaven, and for the love of his own little mother on earth, should handle all womankind gently, and hold them in all honour, and speak small to 'em, and not scare 'em, but go about to come at their love with all manner of homages, and observances, and circumbendibuses."

A little later, he spied Kate, attendant to Maid Marian who was the daughter of Sir Richard in this version, picking flowers and singing. He wanted to give her a kiss, but Kate gave him one first. He was surprised and a little affronted because he thought that he should be the one to give the first kiss. When Marian appeared a few moments later, Little John asked her,

> "I am no ruffler, my lady; but I pray you, my lady, if a man and a maid love one another, may the maid give the first kiss?"

To which Marian replied,

> "It will be all the more gracious of her if she do."

In some of the following scenes, Thomas Love Peacock's influence was at work in the characterization of Maid Marian. At the banquet held for

Robin's thirtieth birthday—he was also an earl here—she danced with him but reminded him that she would not give an answer about marriage until King Richard came back to England. Later, when dancing with the sheriff, she told him the very same.

Upon leaving the banquet, her unwavering optimism is apparent. She told Robin, "Till better times," but he wondered, "... if better times should never come?"

> "Then I shall be no worse," Marian said.
> Robin retorted, "And if the worst time come?"
> To which Marian replied, "Why, then I will be better than the time."

Robin gave her a betrothal ring and she promised she would wear it and never part with it. A short time later, Marian was assaulted by Prince John and she fled into the woods with her father. However, she had dressed as a man and when she came upon Robin Hood, he believed her to be her brother. That is, until he challenged her to combat and she refused. But he pressed her to fight on the following day, to which she relented and gave him her glove as confirmation.

But when Marian removed her glove, Robin Hood saw the ring he had given her. At first, he thought that her brother had stolen it from her, but then Marian revealed herself. They pledged their love to one another, but Marian remained steadfast in her chastity, refusing even to kiss Robin Hood. Yet she and Kate stayed with the foresters for a while, even though her father's health was declining.

Marian was so loyal and caring for her father, that she eventually agreed to marry the sheriff whom she did not love, so that her father's debt would be paid, and his lands restored. However, this would only happen if King Richard did not return to save her from such a fate, which he did, as in most Robin Hood stories. Even before that, though, Marian had a change of heart as Prince John and the sheriff both pursued her:

> You, prince, our King to come—you that dishonour
> The daughters and the wives of your own faction—
> Who hunger for the body, not the soul—
> This gallant prince would have me of his—what?
> Household? or shall I call it by that new term
> Brought from the sacred East, his harem? Never,
> Tho' you should queen me over all the realms
> Held by King Richard, could I stoop so low
> As mate with one that holds no love is pure,
> No friendship sacred, values neither man
> Nor woman save as tools—God help the mark!—
> To his own unprincely ends. And you, you, sheriff,
>
> [*Turning to the* sheriff.]
>
> Who thought to buy your marrying me with gold,
> Marriage is of the soul, not of the body.
> Win me you cannot, murder me you may,
> And all I love, Robin, and all his men,
> For I am one with him and his; but while
> I breathe Heaven's air, and Heaven looks down on me,
> And smiles at my best meanings, I remain
> Mistress of mine own self and mine own soul.

So, the tides began to change again with Tennyson's play. But it is still interesting that at that time, female writers were still not taking Maid Marian and adapting her to stories. Perhaps this was because, even at her strongest, she was never really her own woman. She was always seen in relation to Robin Hood, whether as his lady love or his wife.

So, while she was not constrained as much as other fictional female characters in the Victorian era, she was not actually an ideal icon who appealed to women writers. That is, until times began to change and more modern authors—including some female ones—finally started to write about her.

Chapter Ten

Maid Marian in 20th Century Literature

After literacy became a privilege for everyone and not just the elite, more and more books were published. That meant more and more adaptations of the everlasting folktales and legends, too. There have been so many writers who were inspired by Robin Hood—probably more than one could read in a lifetime!

In the first half of the 1900s, many of the texts surrounding the forest outlaw were written for children. Some of them had breathtaking illustrations, such as *Robin Hood* by Paul Creswick, published by David McKay in 1917 and including images by the renowned illustrator N. C. Wyeth (Creswick, 2016). But the result of making the legend appeal to—and appropriate for—children was that Maid Marian was absent from several of the retellings. However, when she did appear, she again provided a stark example of how the world had transformed.

For also as we reached the 20th century, the roles of women, in Western society in any case, gradually began to change. Naturally then, the heroines of literature, such as Maid Marian, began to reflect this shift in culture. Sometimes, she was depicted as she was in the old ballads—as Robin Hood's equal in combat and archery and righteous spirit. At other times, she was the real leader of the Sherwood band. And in a few stories, Robin Hood himself was reimagined as a woman.

So, it is time to look at some of the books in which Maid Marian plays a key role, or even stars as the lead of her own story.

Before Roger Lancelyn Green, E. Charles Vivian collected the many old ballads and plays based on the Robin Hood saga and put them all together in a rewritten novel format. His first book, *The Adventures of Robin Hood*, came out in 1906 (Vivian, 1965) and he also wrote another, *Robin Hood and His Merry Men*, published two decades later and republished in 1995 (Vivian, 1995). Maid Marian played a similar role in these books as she did in Green's—both as a companion and feminine counterpart to Robin Hood, as well as a character with her own personality.

Among the first of the female authors to take up the character and reinvent her was Amy Ella Blanchard. In 1908, her twelve-chapter children's book, *Little Maid Marian,* appeared on the shelves (Blanchard, 2019) but this was not a story about our heroine. Rather, the young Marian about whom Blanchard wrote was a little girl of the Victorian age, raised by her grandparents in America after her mother died and her father stayed in Berlin. She went to school and made some friends, played with her pets Tippy and Dippy, and grew frustrated at the lack of freedom she had under her grandparents' care. However, this little Maid Marian shared the strong will—and appreciation of nature—of her namesake.

Four years later, we had Henry Gilbert's retelling of the old legend, *Robin Hood*, which returned us to the Nottingham and Sherwood of the Middle Ages (Davies, 2018). Though Maid Marian was only briefly mentioned in his version, she was not portrayed as just a damsel in distress, but was a strong female character, particularly for the time in which he was writing.

Women in America were fighting for new rights throughout the first few decades of the 1900s and were gaining new opportunities. Those inclined to storytelling were seeing their books in print—and no longer had to use a male pseudonym on the cover. One of these was Edith Heal, who, in 1928, sent her book *Robin Hood* to the press (Heal, 1928). It was the classic story retold for audiences of her day, and by a woman. So, it was hopefully marketed for a wider audience than some of the similar books that specifically targeted boys.

In 1934, Geoffrey Trease wrote a much-loved reinterpretation of Robin Hood titled *Bows Against the Barons* (Trease, 1973). The main character was sixteen-year-old Dickon, a peasant boy who fled into Sherwood and joined Robin Hood's band after killing one of the king's deer. While well-written at a good pace for young readers, *Bows Against the Barons* barely mentioned Maid Marian. She played only a very minor role as companion to the leader of the outlaws.

Rosemary Sutcliff wrote books in several different genres, including children's books, historical fiction and material for radio, television, and films (Lawton, 2018). She adapted the classic story of Robin Hood in her first book *The Chronicles of Robin Hood* which was initially published in 1950 with illustrations by C. Walter Hodges (Sutcliff, 2013). This work launched her career as an author of children's stories and retellings of myths and folktales.

In the middle of the 20th century, T. H. White produced a series of short novels, collected together as *The Once and Future King* (White, 1962). The first part is called *The Sword in the Stone* and is about the young boy nicknamed The Wart, who would grow up to become the legendary King Arthur.

So, how is *The Once and Future King* of relevance to Maid Marian and Robin Hood? Both are characters in the text of *The Sword in the Stone*. Arthur and his stepbrother Kay encountered the couple, named as Robin Wood (according to this tale, the real name of the man known as Robin Hood) and his wife Marian when they entered the Forest Sauvage. Marian was a capable fighter and excelled at hunting, and she and Robin Wood taught the boys some skills, as well as helping them to save the people who had been kidnapped by the treacherous Morgan le Fay.

So, from this point on, our legendary lady was featured more and more in literature, taking on many different roles and appearing in many different genres from romance to fantasy.

Locksley by Nicholas Chase appeared on shelves in 1984 and, in the pages of this unique twist on the legend, we saw Marian not as Robin Hood's lady love, but as his sister (Chase, 1984). Marian was, in fact, the lover of Little John, though she eventually became a nun. She was an important figure in the novel, even though she was not Robin Hood's sweetheart. There was, however, a romance for Robin Hood amidst all the medieval politics. Locksley was appointed the protector of Princess Berengaria, who was King Richard's betrothed. And he fell in love with Berengaria, who was nicknamed Gala. At some point, Marian and Gala traded places after King Richard died, so that Gala could be near to Robin Hood. For a unique reimagining, this one seemed to be well-liked, though it is missing from a lot of Robin Hood book lists, maybe because it is so different from the traditional story.

The next book to be considered also diverged a little bit but kept many of the old familiar elements found in the earlier works about Robin Hood. First published in 1988, *The Outlaws of Sherwood* by Robin McKinley contained the characters we have come to know from previous stories as well as some new characters, including other women, who were the author's own invention (McKinley, 1988).

McKinley depicted Robin as fleeing into Sherwood Forest after accidentally killing someone who shot an arrow at him. Marian and Robin's friend Much convinced him to become an outlaw and many more people who were struggling under Norman rule joined him. One of these was Alan-a-dale who wanted to rescue Marjorie, the woman he loved, from an arranged marriage to a corrupt baron. Likewise, Will Scarlet's sister was supposed to wed a Norman nobleman, but it was against her will. She joined the band disguised as a young man named Cecil, before she was revealed to be Cecily Scarlet. Soon afterwards, Cecily and Little John became a couple.

Meanwhile, Marian participated in an archery contest and won. Robin did not go because he realized that the contest was a means to trap him. Guy of Gisbourne attacked Marian because he thought she was Robin Hood in disguise. Fortunately, she was saved by Little John and Cecily who took her to Friar Tuck's hideout to recover. Shortly thereafter, Robin Hood revealed his feelings for Marian and asked for her hand in marriage. The rest, as they say, is history—or at least the fictional history of the tale we are used to. After King Richard returned, he approved the marriage of Marian and Robin and granted Robin the right to inherit his family's lands.

In 1999, another novel hit the market—*Sherwood* by Parke Godwin (Godwin, 1991). Set a century before the traditional tale took place, Edward Denby's father was killed during an uprising against William the Conqueror. Marian had also lost her land and her family when she encountered the man who brought her to Sherwood and became an outlaw. Denby became Robin Hood and fought against the evils that were plaguing his homeland.

Godwin also wrote a sequel, *Robin and the King*, in which the middle-aged Robin, who was now husband to Marian and father of two children, was captured by William the Conqueror and made his slave (Godwin, 1993). He needed to find a way to escape in this novel filled with medieval politics, battle action, and strange superstitions.

The romanticism of the Robin Hood tale was really emphasized in *The Thief's Mistress* (Feyrer, 1996). Written by Gayle Feyrer in 1996, this version is a historical romance and, on its cover, reads: "A prince of thieves. A passionate maiden. A love so powerful it became a legend."

Feyrer portrayed a delightfully spirited Marian who was robbed by a group of bandits as she passed through Sherwood Forest, though Robin only stole a kiss from her and nothing else. She was immediately enraged but, despite this, was overcome by desire for him. This seriously complicated matters because Sir Guy of Guisborne was also courting her. The ensuing story has all the tropes you would expect from a romance novel, but there was also a surprising level of historical fact contained within its pages.

The 1990s were big for Maid Marian. Firstly, there was Theresa Tomlinson's book, *The Forestwife*, which was originally published in 1993 (Tomlinson, 1995). This was a young adult novel featuring teenager Mary de Holt, whose mother had died in childbirth, so she had been raised by her uncle, Lord

Holt. When she was promised in marriage to a much older man, she fled to the forest, followed closely by her faithful nurse, Agnes.

Agnes became a midwife and healer in the greenwood—a forest wife. She taught Mary, who became Marian, how to survive in nature and use herbs to heal. As they encountered other people in the woods, including many other female characters who were new to the story, it was revealed that Agnes had a son, Robert, who was destined to become the outlaw hero Robin Hood.

The novel had some interesting plot twists and included pagan elements, such as a May Day festival. Most readers found it sweet, if a little slow at times, but many readers did not like the use of Shakespearean style dialogue. The sequels that were written, *Child of the May* and *The Path of the She Wolf*, featured other prominent characters (Tomlinson, 1998, 2000). Theresa Tomlinson was certainly not the first nor would be the last author to give Maid Marian a leading role.

Another modern retelling is to be found in *Lady of the Forest: A Novel of Sherwood*, which was written by Jennifer Roberson and published in 1992 by Zebra Books (Roberson, 1992). The story was told from the perspective of several different characters but was really centered on Lady Marian FitzWalter, an English noblewoman.

This tale was written as a prequel to the familiar legend because Roberson wanted to craft a more defined story of the origin of the characters who populated Sherwood. She wanted to show how "seven very different people from a rigidly stratified social structure came to join together to fight the inequities of medieval England" (Wikipedia, 2023j). She spent a full year researching and writing the historical fiction book and blended facts from history with fictional imaginings.

The story began with Lady Marian FitzWalter attending a festival at the Earl of Huntington's castle which was being held in honor of the return of the Earl's only surviving son, Lord Robert of Locksley, who had just arrived home from the Crusades. Unfortunately, Lady Marian's father, Sir Hugh

FitzWalter, had been murdered by Saracens during the battle, and she asked Robert to tell her what happened. He reacted very strongly when he had to recall the events, and in modern times, this would probably be attributed to some sort of post-traumatic stress disorder.

However, Robert did tell Lady Marian that her father wished her to marry William DeLacey, the Sheriff of Nottingham. To complicate matters, Prince John announced his plan to marry Robert to his illegitimate daughter, Joanna.

Not long after the festival, Lady Marian was in the market with the sheriff, when she was abducted by William "Scarlet" Scathlocke and dragged deep into Sherwood Forest. Lord Robert tracked them and convinced Scarlet to release Marian once he found them. On the way back to her home, Robert fell ill with a fever and Lady Marian nursed him back to health and helped him to work through some of his mental torment.

They grew closer, with Robert comparing her with Helen of Troy and saying that many men desired her. Lady Marian was disbelieving of her own beauty, but became more frightened of the sheriff, who still had intentions to force her hand. Eventually, Robert and Lady Marian fell in love. Their affection was tender and passionate and at one point, Marian was compelled to touch him, to feel his arm and know the warmth and vitality beneath the tunic sleeve. She needed to be sure that he was alive, breathing, and hers.

Robert began to help the people of Nottingham by stealing from the wealthy aristocrats to feed them and to collect ransom money for King Richard. He and Lady Marian had to flee to the small village of Locksley after she refused the sheriff one more time. There, she was found and apprehended and taken to the sheriff's dungeon. Once imprisoned, she was told that she would be charged with witchcraft if she did not marry the sheriff.

Just in time, Robert and his friends came to Lady Marian's rescue. But they were seized by Prince John and his cronies and were about to be arrested when another convenient appearance was made. It was King Richard! As in the older versions of the story, his return marked the happy ending of the novel, as he granted them all a royal pardon.

However, Roberson wasn't done with these characters yet. She wrote a sequel to *Lady of the Forest* in 1999, titled *Lady of Sherwood*. This one started with the death of King Richard and Prince John vying for the throne against his young nephew, Arthur of Brittany (Wikipedia, 2023i). Once again, Lady Marian, Robin, and their allies found themselves antagonized by William DeLacey, the Sheriff of Nottingham. Of course, their pardon was no longer legitimate, so that put them in mortal danger.

At this point, Robin and Lady Marian were lovers and had been living together at her manor, Ravenskeep. But Lady Marian, after several miscarriages, realized that she could not have children. She hid this information from Robin because she did not want him to worry about her. Instead, she told his father and asked him to demand that Robin leave her so that he could become a father with someone else.

With the pardon now being null and void, the sheriff renewed his efforts to arrest the outlaws of Sherwood. He attacked Ravenskeep and tried to have the manor legally removed from Marian's ownership. She declared war on the sheriff but eventually she lost everything and retreated with Robin and the other outlaws to the forest. Then, Marian and Robin were finally married.

Although Roberson claimed she found it difficult to depict medieval women, her work was lauded. Stephen Knight called her take an interesting one that really elevated Lady Marian's character (Wikipedia, 2023j). In turn, he felt "it is evident that Roberson is using the post-Vietnam mood as the basis for her weakening of Robin to permit a 'strong woman' presentation of Marian." And Jane Tolmie wrote in an article published by the *Journal of Gender Studies*, that *Lady of the Forest* was just one more in a long line of novels of the period that had women being forced to endure acts of violence and oppression "as aspects of a continuum rather than as isolated difficulties" (Wikipedia, 2023j). So, what would the new millennium bring?

Chapter Eleven

Maid Marian in 21st Century Literature

The next writer to be inspired by the legendary heroine was Elsa Watson. She published her novel, *Maid Marian*, in 2005, after realizing that very many people knew the name of the character but little else about her (Watson, 2004).

The overview of Watson's book reads: "An irresistible reimagining of the Robin Hood legend, *Maid Marian* brings to life the rollicking—and romantic—world of the Middle Ages." It was told from the point of view of Norman orphan Marian Fitzwater, who was wed to Lord Hugh of Sencaster when they were both only five years old. By the time she was seventeen, though, Lord Hugh had mysteriously died. This made her the ward of King Richard the Lionheart.

But Richard was away fighting in the Crusades, as per usual. So, his mother, Queen Eleanor of Aquitaine, took charge of Marian. Whoever the queen would select to be Marian's husband would come into possession of her lands. So, it was all political and not about love, just as it always had been for the girl.

Well, Marian had had enough, and not wanting to be married off to another deemed suitable by Queen Eleanor, sought the outlaw Robin Hood in Sherwood Forest, hoping he could save her from such a marriage. Since

Robin Hood was a Saxon, the pair did not hit it off immediately, but she was taken by his kindness and his handsome features. After finding out, with Robin's help, that she was to be married to her late husband's brother, Lady Marian feared for her safety, as several members of that family had already died mysteriously. Fortunately, on the eve of her wedding, Robin arrived and took her back to the forest, where they planned ways to recover her lands and expose the treacherous plots of their enemies.

The book received mixed reviews, with the consensus seeming to be that Watson really nailed the character of Robin Hood but that her villains were too comical, instead of being threatening. Nevertheless, it was good to see Lady Marian front and center in a retelling.

In 2007, *Hood,* the first of a trilogy of books by Stephen R. Lawhead called *The King Raven Trilogy,* was published (Lawhead, 2007). The characters from the Robin Hood legend were taken from their traditional site of Sherwood and were placed in Wales.

Not only was the setting completely changed, so were the figures. The Robin Hood representation came in the form of Bran in *Hood*, the first book in the series. The next two books were *Scarlet* and *Tuck,* focusing on Will Scarlet and Friar Tuck respectively (Lawhead, 2008, 2009). Some other figures from the legend, including Marian, made an appearance, but their characterizations were very limited.

Another young adult version is Kathryn Lasky's *Hawksmaid: The Untold Story of Robin Hood and Maid Marian,* first published as an electronic book in 2010 (Lasky, 2010). The young woman protagonist was called Matty before she became Maid Marian, and she was the daughter of one of the most famous falconers in England. Matty eventually gained the ability to hear the thoughts of the falcons and speak their language.

Her friend Fynn was outlawed when the Sheriff of Nottingham became the new authority in the town, and Fynn then transformed into the hero

Chapter Eleven

Robin Hood. And Robin Hood needed Matty and her bird, Marigold, to help him save the people from starvation and suffering. There was a lot of action, intrigue, and romance in this iteration of the tale. The forest setting really came to life, almost as a character in its own right. Matty described how she felt upon coming into the forest. She said it was as though she was enveloped in a delicate golden light as soon as she walked in. It surrounded her like a bright mist. Everything seemed to be new as if it were a different universe.

Angus Donald also penned a series inspired by the medieval tale. *Outlaw: A Novel of Robin Hood* was his first book with elements of the legend but much grittier in tone (Donald, 2011). The character in possession of Robin's heart was Marie-Anne, who retained both her nobility and chastity from the older versions. Donald described his book as "a gripping, action-packed historical thriller that delves deep into the fascinating legend of Robin Hood."

Of course, the romance genre was just ripe to tell more tales about the character of Maid Marian. Deb Stover wrote a version in 2013 that is set in Oklahoma in the 1890s, *Maid Marian and the Lawman* (Stover, 2013). Her main character was Mary Goode, who had a brother named Robin whom she rescued from an institution, together with two others.

The three young men were so inspired by Robin Hood that they committed some actual robberies, and this brought a U.S. Marshal, Shane Latimer, after them. He was enchanted by Mary after he came under her care when his horse was spooked and threw him. But he also had a duty to bring in the thieves whom he had been sent to apprehend. So, as you can imagine, Shane and Mary developed feelings for one another and needed to find a way to resolve their conflict to be together.

Then came a very big departure from the chaste maiden who pledged to remain virginal until King Richard returned and married her to Robin Hood. Colette Gale put out a three-book series called *Seduced Classics* in which she retold three classic stories with a steamy twist. Her version of the

Robin Hood legend was *Bound by Honor: An Erotic Novel of the Robin Hood Legend* (Gale, 2014).

In this unique book, Marian was Lady of Leaford and was sent to Prince John's Court of Pleasure by the queen to spy on him. While attempting to navigate the "carnal temptations" of the court, she also felt a growing desire for both the forest outlaw Robin Hood and the cold, mysterious Sheriff of Nottingham. This 2014 text, although fiction, is an example of the leaps and bounds women have made in more recent times toward sexual freedom and freedom of expression.

The years 2019 to 2022 were turbulent ones for the world as people dealt with the coronavirus pandemic. Amongst all those confined to their homes during lockdown were writers who decided to revisit the legend of Robin Hood and tell more stories inspired by the medieval legend.

M.T. Boulton decided to base the story on a "what if" thought. Namely, what if Marian married Guy, rather than Robin? *The Outlaws of Nottingham* tells the outcome, with *The Warriors of Sherwood* being the first volume of the epic trilogy (Boulton, 2019).

Another set of three books is Olivia Longueville and J. C. Plummer's *Robin Hood Trilogy* published between 2018 and 2021. In the first part of the saga, *Robin Hood's Dawn*, the character of Robin Fitzooth, Earl of Huntingdon was convicted of a terrible crime that he did not commit (Longueville & Plummer, 2018). He fled into Sherwood to avoid punishment. There, he led a band of men against the villainous Sheriff of Nottingham and his henchmen and began to unravel a network of betrayal that threatened to destroy the English Royal Family.

The second book in the series is titled *Robin Hood's Widow* (Longueville & Plummer, 2020). In this story, Marian took center stage. She was devastated when Guy of Gisborne supposedly killed her husband, Robin Hood, but she found a new purpose in life that eclipsed the heartache of widowhood.

Assuming the role of leader of the men who had previously followed Robin, she was relentless in her efforts to protect his legacy and in her quest for vengeance.

Then, in the final book, *Robin Hood's Return*, Robin actually came back—alive—from the Crusades, only to be outlawed (Longueville & Plummer, 2021). So, Robin and Marian continued their fight against the Sheriff of Nottingham and faced the wrath of Queen Eleanor who was collecting a king's ransom to secure the release of the captured King Richard the Lionheart. The couple worked together to prove their innocence and foil a malevolent plan by the King of France and his evil advisor to end the Plantagenet dynasty forever.

The Ghosts of Sherwood is Carrie Vaughn's 2020 novella about the three children of Robin Hood and Maid Marian (Vaughn, 2020a). The story took place almost two decades after the traditional legend where Robin and Marian were married. There is sixteen-year-old Mary, a skilled archer, her brother John, with whom she often spats, and sister Eleanor, who does not speak.

The conflicts that surrounded Mary's possible arranged marriage, and the danger the family might have been in since Prince John had taken the throne, were over-shadowed when the children were kidnapped. The following plot is a fast-paced, light read, and this book was followed by a sequel, *Heirs of Locksley* (Vaughn, 2020b). King John was now dead, and the new monarch was his son, King Henry III, who inherited the throne at age thirteen. The Locksley children befriended King Henry and uncovered sinister plots in the adventurous sequel.

Around the same time, Meagan Spooner released her novel, which also took place long after the legend. In *Sherwood*, Robin of Locksley had passed away and Maid Marian grieved deeply for her loss (Spooner, 2019). But then she took up the mantle as head protector of the people of Nottingham because they were still in dire need of protection from the Sheriff. Of course, Guy of Gisborne wanted to step into Robin's shoes and make Marian his bride, but she had other ideas.

Jenny Elder Moke decided to make Marian's daughter, Isabelle, the main character of her novel, *Hood*, which was published by Disney-Hyperion in 2021 (Moke, 2021). Marian told Isabelle that she had the blood of kings and rebels within her, before sending her away from the convent where she was raised and into the forest to find her father, Robin Hood. There, she had to find her place within his band and survive the nefarious plans of the people who wanted her and her parents dead.

Also in 2021, Tilman Roehrig decided to tell the ancient story from Little John's point of view. His book was titled *The Shadows of Sherwood Forest,* and the main character was a peasant named John Little, whose foster daughter, Marian, escaped into the forest with him when their village was raided (Roehrig, 2021). But Robin Hood caught and imprisoned them. Over time, though, both Little John, as he became known, and Marian grew to be Robin Hood's friends and confidantes and learned to fight by his side.

In other iterations, Robin Hood isn't exactly a "he." In fact, for the last decade especially, switching his gender has become something of a trend.

Gender-Swapping Robin Hood

Several modern versions of Robin Hood did not focus on Maid Marian as a character, but, still thirsty for a feminine bent, changed the hero to a girl or a woman.

Edale Lane even kept both characters, as Robyn and her best friend Marian found themselves caught up in court intrigues and greenwood adventures—and with each other. *Heart of Sherwood*, the winner of the Best Historical Lesbian Romance of 2018-2019, has really shown how far removed from the original one can get, while still keeping the essence of the legend alive (Lane, 2018).

In *Royal Rebel*, which was released in 2009, Dana Taylor told the tale of King Richard's secret daughter, Princess Robin (Taylor, 2009). She led a group of merry men against the tyrant Prince John. Robin did all she could to fight against the injustices occurring in the country while she waited for her birth father to return from the Crusades. When Sir Simon of Loxley came back to England instead to be King Richard's spy, Robin could not help but fall in love with him, even though he was arrogant and controlling and she was used to being the leader.

K.M. Shea also decided to switch the gender of the hero in *Robyn Hood: A Girl's Tale* and its sequel, *Robyn Hood: Fight for Freedom* (Shea, 2022a, 2022b). Both were independently published but received high reviews for the fun and adventurous spirit, as well as the humor, imbued in the novels.

Shea tells us: "The ballads lie. Robin Hood, the Bold and Brave Outlaw of Sherwood Forest, is a girl." But then she turned that dramatic opening on its head in *Robyn Hood: A Girl's Tale* by letting us know that Robyn fell into the role unwillingly while saving her friend from the Crown's men.

In the second book, *Robyn Hood: Fight for Freedom,* Maid Marian played a larger role. She had been Robyn's childhood friend but when Robyn fled to the courts of Prince John to hide in plain sight, Marian exposed her disguise. The plot is further complicated by the arrival of the merry men to plead for Robyn's release with the subsequent capture of Little John and Will Scarlet. Then, Marian's betrothal to one of Prince John's ghastly retainers was announced. It was up to Robyn to rescue the men and save her friend from a loveless, violent marriage.

A book geared toward younger readers that is set in more modern times is *Shadows of Sherwood: A Robyn Hoodlum Adventure* (Magoon, 2016). This novel by Kekla Magoon stars Robyn Loxley, who, at twelve years old, found herself alone after her parents vanished. She joined a band of misfits in Nott City, which was ruled by a corrupt official named Ignomus Crown whom the kids attempted to thwart at every opportunity. This was just the start of a series of more Robyn Hoodlum adventures that are perfect for pre-teens.

In a similar vein, *The Outlaws of Sherwood Street* by Peter Abrahams is set in present times (Abrahams, 2013). Robbie Forester is the lead character, whose friends Silas, Ashanti, and Tut-Tut help her set things right in the two books of the series. The book is intended for both boys and girls and is a refreshing change from the traditionally gendered middle-grade books on the shelves.

There is also a five-book series *Rowan Hood* by Nancy Springer, published between 2001 and 2005, which featured Robin's estranged daughter Rosemary (Springer, 2001). In this way, it is similar to Springer's popular series, *Enola Holmes*, about the daughter of the famous detective Sherlock Holmes. In the *Rowan Hood* series, Rosemary's mother Celandine was burnt as a witch, so Rosemary disguised herself as a boy, changed her name to Rowan, and fled into the forest to find her father. She was joined by several new characters, including Ettarde, a runaway princess, who was the favorite character of many readers.

And finally we come to C. K. Brooke's young adult adaptation, *Marian, Princess Thief: A Robin Hood retelling,* in which teenage Lady Marian was chased by an assassin into the forest, where she encountered a group of other young women, all outlawed (Brooke, 2019). Over the next few years, Lady Marian and her merry maidens (under the guises of Rob-in-Hood and his merry men) undermined the prince's nefarious plots, stole from the rich to feed the poor, and avoided the Sheriff of Nottingham—that is until they were forced to capture the sheriff and Lady Marian discovered that not everyone was who they seemed to be.

Although there are numerous other representations of Marian and her legendary archer lover, it is not practical to try and list all of them, especially as it is extremely likely that there will be many more stories about our heroine and her lover to come. Indeed, apart from the novels there are also numerous comic books and graphic novels retelling the legend. So, now it is time to consider a different type of medium, that of opera.

Chapter Twelve

Maid Marian in Opera

The grandeur, drama, and emotional intensity of opera make it an ideal medium for delving into Maid Marian's complicated personality. Composers and librettists have a wealth of topics to explore while writing about her narrative, ranging from social justice and political intrigue to love and loyalty. The medium of opera vividly and thrillingly brings Maid Marian's world to life with its arias, passionate duets, and dramatic ensembles.

Of course, Maid Marian has also appeared in musicals and pantomimes, but this chapter will concentrate on opera and will examine five different approaches that librettists and composers have used to interpret Maid Marian's character for the operatic stage.

The first example is *Marian,* a comic opera which opened at the Covent Garden Theatre in London in 1788 and ran for 41 performances. The libretto was by Frances Brooke, an English novelist and playwright and the music was written by William Shields (Brooke, 1789, 1800). His collaboration with Frances Brooke resulted in an *opus* that combined melodious music and a witty dialogue.

The character of Marian was central to the plot. She was portrayed as a young woman who became entangled in several amusing situations involving love, societal conventions and mistaken identity. In this opera, her love interest was a young man called Edward, not Robin Hood. There was indeed a character called Robin who was Marian's father's choice for her husband. This Robin was not an outlaw but ran a lucrative ferry business, owned some acres of land and four cows and had a vote in the country. Eventually, after some plot twists, Edward inherited a large amount of money and was revealed to be a gentleman. Thus, Marian got the man of her dreams and Robin married another young lady.

The next operatic depiction of Maid Marian premiered on October 10, 1822, at the English Opera House, London, now known as the Lyceum Theatre. Entitled *Maid Marian; or, Huntress of Arlingford*, it was a collaboration between librettist James Robinson Planché and composer Henry Rowley Bishop (Planché & Bishop, 1822). Their opera presented Marian as a bold and independent heroine, leading a band of outlaws in the forest of Arlingford. She was an advocate for justice, standing for resistance against oppression and defending the vulnerable and downtrodden. Marian was also shown as a skilled archer and huntress who embodied femininity and strength in a society ruled by men. She was both a captivating and inspirational personality for audiences because of her unwavering commitment to her principles together with her loyalty to her cause. Planché's lively libretto and Bishop's melodious score captured beautifully Marian's adventurous spirit as she navigated the challenges of medieval England.

The music for *Robin Hood: A romantic English Opera in three acts* was written by George Alexander Macfarren with the libretto by John Oxenford (Fortunaso, n.d.-a). This opera was first produced at Her Majesty's Theatre in London in 1860. It is a fine example of an English Romantic Opera which was the term used to describe Victorian operas of the day which incorporated dialogue interspersed with songs and ensembles instead of *recitative* to advance the plot. It was the fourth of six staged operas that he completed and after it premièred, it was later revived and taken on tour (Victorian Opera Northwest, 2020). Victorian Opera Northwest recorded Macfarren's *Robin Hood* in March 2010, the first performance for more than 100 years (Macfarren & Oxenford, 1860; Victorian Opera Northwest, 2020).

In this opera, Maid Marian was the daughter of the Sheriff of Nottingham and Robin Hood, using the name *Locksley*, was the object of her loving desires. The sheriff was prepared to accept Robin Locksley as his daughter's love provided he could prove his marksmanship skills at a fair to be held the next day. Robin was indeed able to prove his skill and claimed Marian's hand, but he was then recognized as the outlaw and was seized and taken captive.

Marian escaped her apartment and, disguised as a boy, went to the forest and told the outlaws that Robin had been taken and would soon be executed. She led the outlaws to the castle and Robin heard her singing with the merry men. Robin was brought out for his confession to be heard and, using a free arm, summoned his faithful followers with a blast of his horn. They appeared, led by Marian, but were overpowered by the sheriff's men. However, the document which the sheriff thought was the Death Warrant was actually a Pardon from King Richard on the proviso that Robin and his men entered the King's service. The sheriff agreed once again to Marian and Robin's union, and this was followed by general rejoicing.

So, once again, Marian was depicted as an independent, strong woman, prepared to do whatever was necessary to save her man. Her role personified the heroic and romantic aspects of her character as well as her resilience and commitment to Robin Hood.

The next example started its life under the title *Robin Hood*. This was a comic opera by composer Reginald De Koven with lyrics by Harry B. Smith and lyrics for an additional song *Oh Promise Me* by Clement Scott (Wikipedia, 2023t). The opera was based on the Robin Hood legend and took place during the reign of King Richard I (1189-1199 CE). It was written in Chicago, Illinois, in the winter of 1888 to 1889.

Robin Hood made its debut in Chicago on June 9, 1890. It was produced and performed by the Chicago Opera House, often referred to as the *Bostonians*. Then, in 1891, the opera was presented in London at the Prince of Wales Theatre under the revised title *Maid Marian* (Wikipedia, 2023t). This change shifted the spotlight to Maid Marian and provided a new angle to the tale. In 1900, the opera was again presented at the Knickerbocker Theater on Broadway as *Maid Marian* and the opera was also produced at the Chestnut Street Opera House, Philadelphia on 4 November 1901 (The Gilbert and Sullivan Archive, 2017). There were additional revivals under its original title of *Robin Hood* in New York in 1902, 1912, 1918, 1930, 1932 and 1944 (Internet Broadway Database, 2001-2024).

In 1910, at the age of 20, May L. Valentine made her American debut as a conductor of Gilbert and Sullivan opera revivals on the east coast. In 1919, she was working in New York and was approached by Reginald De Koven to conduct the orchestra for a planned revival of *Robin Hood* that was to go on tour on the Chautauqua circuit (King Johnson, 2022). Chautauqua was an adult education and social movement in America that peaked in popularity between the late 19th century and early 20th century (Wikipedia, 2024a). Valentine produced and conducted several popular English language light operas during the period 1922 to 1925 on the Chautauqua circuit (Norling, 2018). Her mission was to present opera to the masses where it had previously been the realm of the elite. She took her commercial touring troupe through at least 47 states of America. It seems fitting that the opera which portrayed Maid Marian as an independent, resourceful and powerful lady, was conducted on tour by the only American woman conductor of operas at that time.

Later, the Ohio Light Opera commissioned Quade Winter, a renowned tenor, to create a new critical edition of the opera, which was presented in

2004. This was based on the composer's original manuscripts found in the Library of Congress. Albany Records released the whole CD recording under the title *Robin Hood* (De Koven, 2004).

De Koven's score bursting with bright tunes evoked beautifully the atmosphere of medieval England, and together with Smith's witty lyrics, showcased Marian's adventures in Sherwood Forest. Portrayed as a strong and independent woman, Marian played a crucial role in Robin Hood's adventures. This depiction challenged the traditional gender roles of the time and added depth to her character. The cheeky and mischievous side of her personality was also revealed as she outwitted the Sheriff of Nottingham and won the heart of Robin Hood.

Although *Robin Hood* was categorized as a comic opera, it explored more serious themes such as social inequality and justice. This resulted in a work whose layers of complexity to the narrative made it more than a mere light-hearted entertainment piece.

More recently, an opera called *Maid Marian* with music by Colin Macleod Campbell and libretto by his wife Nancy has offered a contemporary approach to the legendary figure. Colin Macleod Campbell was an accomplished Scottish conductor, composer and lecturer who was born in Argyll in 1890 and died in London in 1953. He wrote a successful one act opera, *Thais and Talmaae*, which premiered in 1921. He wrote the music for *Maid Marian* much later. This work was in rehearsal for its planned première in 1938 (Campbell & Campbell, c 1938) but unfortunately, the performance did not eventuate due to the fallout from the Munich Agreement (Holocaust Encyclopedia, n.d.).

In 1955, the stage director T.C. Fairbairn who was a friend of the composer and his family, persuaded the Dundee Opera Company to produce the Campbell opera *Maid Marian*. The opera finally premièred in Dundee on 12 March 1956 at the Gaumont Theatre, three years after the composer's death (Opera Scotland, n.d.). This was a significant event as it marked one of the first times an opera composed by a Scot was performed in Scotland. This signaled a growing appreciation for homegrown talent and paved the way for future Scottish composers.

The newspaper *The Courier* provided an enthusiastic review, stating that the musical score was "melodious". Ballet music in the opera included Maypole and Morris dances, possibly written to evoke Merrie England.

The plot revolved around the romantic relationship between Robin Hood and Maid Marian amidst political unrest. The opera portrayed their courage, loyalty and undying love for each other. It showcased their ongoing struggle against the oppressive Sheriff of Nottingham, their efforts to aid the poor, and their fight for justice. Maid Marian was presented as a strong-willed woman who actively joined Robin Hood's outlaw activities.

Maid Marian's significance in opera is in her complex persona and capacity to elicit strong emotional responses from audiences. She defies traditional gender norms as a powerful, independent heroine who awes audiences with her bravery and tenacity. Her story is made more passionate and intriguing by her romance with Robin Hood, and her struggle for freedom and justice touches on universal themes of hope and redemption.

In conclusion, Maid Marian's attractive persona and romantic appeal are what make her relevant in opera. Her connections to history and folklore give rise to her emotional depth and enable her ability for social commentary. Over ages and cultural boundaries, opera has drawn inspiration from timeless legends such as that of Maid Marian and this should guarantee her continued presence on the operatic stage.

Chapter Thirteen

Maid Marian in the Movies

As technology developed over time, it was inevitable that Maid Marian would be taken from the page and the stage and put on the screen. All great characters are, and, as we have seen, she is one of the greatest.

Over the years, she has appeared in dozens of films and television shows. Just like her literary evolution, her persona on-screen transformed from production to production, based on the time, the scriptwriters, and the directors. Of course, the different actresses who played her also had a huge impact on how she was presented to audiences.

The First Major Robin Hood Movie

The first lucky actress to portray Maid Marian in a major film adaptation was Enid Bennett in the 1922 silent movie *Robin Hood* (Wright, 2022*)*. Bennett was an Australian actress whose work was mostly in silent films in America. Her role of Marian, which was perhaps her most famous, was opposite Douglas Fairbanks' Robert, Earl of Huntingdon—the character who would become the outlaw Robin Hood.

In fact, the full title under which the film was copyrighted is *Douglas Fairbanks in Robin Hood* (Wikipedia, 2023e). This motion picture based on the legend of Robin Hood was expensive to make and was the first to have a Hollywood première.

Douglas Fairbanks in Robin Hood had a reported budget of one million dollars, making it one of the costliest films of the 1920s. It was shot at the Pickford-Fairbanks Studio which Fairbanks owned together with his wife, Mary Pickford, and was distributed by United Artists. The set was huge—a castle and village were constructed on a grand scale, with Frank Lloyd Wright, the famous architect, designing specific elements.

Fortunately, the film was a hit with audiences. It was also the highest-grossing film of its day. Fairbanks himself was only two years out from his role as the lead character in *The Mark of Zorro*, so he was cementing himself as a swashbuckling hero in people's minds. In fact, this Robin Hood motion picture was produced by his own company, Douglas Fairbanks Pictures Corporation, and Fairbanks was the one who adapted the script for the film medium under his alias Elton Thomas.

Since this was the first time audiences would be seeing the folk hero on the big screen, it established many of the story elements that audiences would expect to see in later depictions. And Maid Marian, as Lady Marian Fitzwalter, had an important part to play in the plot.

The film began with a title sequence that explained the setting, appropriately described in a romantic way, together with a form of disclaimer about the blending of factual history and embellished legend:

> *"So fleet the works of men,*
> *Back to their earth again;*
> *Ancient and Holy things*
> *Fade like a dream.*

Chapter Thirteen

Stately castles whose turrets pierced the sky have left imperishable record ~

Though the storms of centuries have laid waste to the works of men their spirit soars on and poets make live again the days of chivalry.

Mediaeval England ~ England in the Age of Faith. Her chronicles tell of warriors and statesmen, of Royal Crusaders, of jousting knights. Her ballads sing of jolly friars, of troubadours, of gallant outlaws who roamed her mighty forests.

History ~ in its ideal state ~ is a compound of legend and chronicle and from out of both we offer you an impression of the Middle Ages ~
(Wright, 2022)

Like most silent films, it was interspersed with text throughout its duration to explain who the characters were, their dialogue, and what was happening in the story. This version opened with a tournament hosted by King Richard the Lion-Hearted [*sic*], who was enthusiastically munching on a turkey leg while his "sinister, dour" brother, Prince John, watched him in disgust, supposedly contemplating his desire to sit on the throne. Then, our heroine Lady Marian is the third character to be introduced.

She entered the scene with a flock of handmaidens, who were helping her look the part of the queen. Interestingly, she studied herself in a hand mirror after donning a crown, and a few moments later, Robert, Earl of Huntingdon, examined his mustache by looking into his shiny chain mail. There was a definite comedic vibe to the whole film which could possibly be seen as a harbinger for parodies of the legend in the future. But, back to the story.

Lady Marian refused to give her veil to Guy of Gisbourne, who wished to wear it into the tournament, and the Earl of Huntingdon promptly won a joust against him. King Richard was so impressed with the Earl of Huntingdon's skill he decreed that Robert should accompany him on the Holy Crusades as his "second in command."

Though Robert claimed to be "afeared of women," he accepted the chaplet, or wreath, from Lady Marian, and then was chased in the castle by other noble ladies, only escaping by diving into the moat. At the feast that followed, when Robert rushed to Lady Marian's aid as she was fighting off the advances of Guy of Gisbourne, she realized that he was smitten with her. The two shared a tender, affectionate moment, but the Earl of Huntingdon had to leave for the Crusades soon afterward.

Prince John promised Lady Marian's hand to Guy of Gisbourne if he brought back Huntingdon's head. He wanted Guy to ensure that King Richard did not return from the Crusades, so that he could remain in power. Then, he began a reign of cruelty, increasing taxes so much that poverty increased accordingly. He replaced good officials with corrupt ones, such as the Sheriff of Nottingham and had the Earl of Huntingdon's castle burnt to the ground.

Yet, "one woman, braver than the rest," pleaded with the monarch to have mercy on the people of England. When Prince John dismissed her, she sent a message to Robert, Earl of Huntingdon, detailing how everyone was suffering under John's tyrannical rule.

Upon receiving her message, Robert asked King Richard for permission to go back to England, but the king assumed that he was afraid of the upcoming battles and did not allow it. Robert still intended to go, but Guy of Gisbourne interfered and King Richard had Robert imprisoned, thinking he was a deserter.

Meanwhile, Prince John tortured Lady Marian's handmaiden until she revealed the truth—that Lady Marian had sent a message to the Earl of Huntingdon. Prince John stated that "Lady Marian shall pay for this with her life. So much for meddling!"

The handmaiden rushed to tell Lady Marian that she must flee the castle and the two mounted horses and rode into the forest. Prince John sent a band of guards after them, and when they found the handmaiden, she told them that Lady Marian's horse threw her and she fell down a cliff, where she was dashed on the rocks below. The same story was told to Robert on his return to England after he escaped from prison with help from his allies. Halfway through the movie, he "began a new life—a life dedicated to revenge—bitter—but joyous."

Now he fully became Robin Hood and called for brave men to join his band of rebels in Sherwood Forest. From this base, he, together with Little John, Will Scarlett, and Allan-a-Dale, tormented Prince John and the Sheriff of Nottingham, regularly invading the castle, stealing gold, and distributing it to the poor. One day, he brought a bag of gold to a priory of nuns and there he was reunited with Lady Marian, who had been in hiding.

At the Crusades, Guy of Gisbourne believed he had stabbed King Richard in his sleep, but in fact, he had stabbed the king's jester. As he headed back to England, Prince John's spies realized that Lady Marian was still alive. The prince wanted nothing more than to take down Robin Hood, so he used this to his advantage, demanding of his guards to "Seize that wench. Drag her here. She shall die the death I promised."

Lady Marian was abducted from the priory and imprisoned in the castle as Robin Hood took over Nottingham Town. Prince John's guards were thwarted as they attempted to attack the band of outlaws in Sherwood Forest, and soon afterward, a mysterious knight came to the merry men in search of Robin Hood.

But he had raced off to save his lady love, having finally received the news of her kidnapping. And he got to her in the nick of time, for as he fought off the guards at the castle, Lady Marian was threatening to throw herself out of the window of her tower rather than give in to Guy of Gisbourne. When she fell, Robin Hood caught her as he climbed the vines on the castle wall. After ensuring that Lady Marian was safe, he engaged in a sword fight with Sir Guy.

Once Guy was defeated, Robin Hood told Lady Marian that his men were coming to the castle, but he also gave her a dagger to use if they failed in their attack on Prince John. He was swiftly captured by the guards and tied to a post. As Lady Marian prepared to plunge the dagger into her heart, Robin Hood's band arrived and—led by the mysterious knight—took over the castle.

The mysterious knight was King Richard who saved Robin Hood from the deathly blows of forty arrows, then revealed himself. As he took back the throne, Robin Hood and Marian were married and, as they say, everyone lived happily ever after.

After the mostly positive reviews that the movie received, a sequel was made titled *Richard the Lion-Hearted*. This starred the same actor, Wallace Beery, who played King Richard in *Robin Hood*. Another fun fact is that Alan Hale Sr., who played Little John, would go on to play the same role in two more films about the legend: *The Adventures of Robin Hood* in 1938 and *Rogues of Sherwood Forest* in 1950 (Wikipedia, 2023ah).

In *Rogues of Sherwood Forest,* the main character was Robin, Earl of Huntingdon, Robin Hood's son (IMDb, 2023e). Marian's character was replaced by a beautiful and young ward of King John, Lady Marianne de Beaudray, played by Diana Lynn. She helped Robin escape from prison. Then, Robin decided to take refuge in Sherwood Forest where he enlisted the help of the now aging merry men as well as common people who were tired of the huge tax burden imposed by King John.

Unfortunately, the film did not have good reviews. It was described as an "uninspired re-telling" with "all the right ingredients but fails to come to life." However, "the costumes and scenery and brilliant Technicolor" stole the show.

Chapter Fourteen

The Adventures of Robin Hood

In 1995, nearly sixty years after its release, *The Adventures of Robin Hood* was deemed "culturally, historically, or aesthetically significant" by the Library of Congress in the United States and was chosen for preservation by the National Film Registry. It is, indeed, the quintessential Robin Hood film that people know best (Wikipedia, 2023b).

The movie came out in 1938 from Warner Brothers Pictures. Like its predecessor, *The Adventures of Robin Hood* was expensive to make, costing $2 million. It was the most expensive film that Warner Brothers had produced at that time. It was also their first foray into Technicolor, although the film had initially been planned as a black and white offering.

Norman Reilly Raine and Seton I. Miller were credited as writers, but the first version of the script was penned by Rowland Leigh. Despite its serving as the foundation for the film, the script was not well received by the studio (Myers, circa 1938). The musical score by composer Erich Wolfgang Korngold won an Academy Award. It also established a style that would be used in many Hollywood action films from then on.

Hal B. Wallis, the head of production at the studio, had to be persistent in his efforts to hire Korngold. At first, the famous opera composer did not want to work on the movie, but finally agreed. Another reason that he took the job in America was because he was worried about the Nazi influence in his home country of Austria. Korngold was correct to be concerned, since not long after he reached America, Austria was annexed.

Another man who made a considerable contribution to the film was Howard Hill. He was a professional archer who shot all the arrows that were included in the final cut, and he also played the role of Elwen the Welshman.

Other stunt actors were employed as well, though the man who played Robin Hood did most of his own stunts. Who was he? Errol Flynn of course. Famous for his roles as swashbuckling heroes, Flynn was an Australian-American actor who lived from 1909 to 1959. He became the literal face of Robin Hood for the audience of his generation and went on to act in many more films.

Basil Rathbone was cast as Guy of Gisbourne. Rathbone would go on to play Sherlock Homes in more than a dozen films over the next seven years. Claude Rains, whose portrayal of villains was often admired, was Prince John. Then there was the lovely and talented Olivia de Haviland, one of the leading actresses of the Golden Age of Hollywood, playing Lady Marian, ward of King Richard.

Dame Olivia Mary de Haviland had an illustrious career. She was in 49 feature films and won several awards. In fact, she and her sister, Joan Fontaine, are the only sibling pair to have won major Academy Awards for acting. Both de Haviland and Flynn starred in *Captain Blood* a couple years before signing on for *The Adventures of Robin Hood* and would act together in future films as well.

The background of the story was a little different in this iteration of the legend, as described by the text at the beginning of the film:

Chapter Fourteen

In the year of Our Lord 1191 when Richard, the Lion-Heart, set forth to drive the infidels from the Holy Land, he gave the Regency of his Kingdom to his trusted friend, Longchamps, instead of to his treacherous brother, Prince John.

Bitterly resentful, John hoped for some disaster to befall Richard so that he, with the help of the Norman barons, might seize the throne for himself. And then on a luckless day for the Saxons...

The scene opened with a town crier telling the people in the village that King Richard was taken by Leopold of Austria, who was holding him prisoner. Ecstatic, Prince John declared himself regent. He immediately began raising taxes and enforcing laws and regulations—such as not killing a deer in the king's forest—saying that it was to accumulate money for King Richard's ransom.

He also celebrated his newfound power during a banquet, where we met Lady Marian for the first time. She was the royal ward of the court, and Prince John knew that the Norman, Sir Guy of Gisbourne, was in love with her. He would like nothing more than for Marian to marry Guy, so that he could stay in the man's good graces and have an ally in his despicable schemes. Lady Marian said that she would appreciate getting to know Guy better before any marriage and Prince John remarked that she was "a very wise woman."

Their meal was interrupted by the arrival of our green-clad hero, Sir Robin of Locksley. In this iteration of the story, he was a Saxon, and a rebel against the current authority, being loyal to King Richard. He was also a self-declared "protector of the people." For that, he was seen by the Norman aristocracy as impudent. Prince John calls him "a bold rascal" and a "saucy fellow" and introduced him to our heroine: "Sir Robin, this is Milady Marian Fitzwalter."

It was not love at first sight, though. When Robin stated that he hoped Lady Marian had a pleasant journey from London, she replied: "What you hope can hardly be important."

"Tsk, tsk. What a pity her manners don't match her looks, Your Highness," Robin said with a twinkle in his eye. He was indeed a cheeky character. When Prince John invited him to sit down and feast with him and the other nobility, Robin obeyed gladly, reminding them all that the Saxons had little to eat. He then confirmed that they were overtaxed and overworked to which Lady Marian said, "Why, you speak treason." To which Robin replied, "Fluently."

Proving Prince John's claim of boldness, he then went on to say that the prince was a traitor and that he, Robin, would do everything in his power to fight against him. After narrowly escaping from the castle, Robin rode into Sherwood Forest, not before sending arrows into some of his pursuers.

Soon afterward, Prince John decreed Robin to be an outlaw, condemned to death. He also stated that anyone who aided him was at risk of being hanged as punishment and ensured that his castles and land were forfeited to the crown.

Over the ensuing days, Robin Hood gathered the Saxons and expanded his band, introducing both Little John and Friar Tuck after humorous meeting scenes with them both. The merry men ambushed a group of Normans as they traveled through Sherwood with luxuries and supplies. The group included Sir Guy of Gisbourne, the Sheriff of Nottingham, and Lady Marian, with her handmaiden, Bess.

Guy promised Robin Hood that he would hang for what he had done. Robin said, "Hanging would be a small price to pay for the company of such a charming lady."

Lady Marian still had not warmed much to our hero, though, wondering, "What can a Saxon hedge robber know of charm *or* ladies?"

Chapter Fourteen

Robin Hood led them all to his camp, where they engaged in a woodland feast. Lady Marian was scornful of the merriment, but Robin convinced her to eat a little. He also proved how loyal his band was to King Richard when they stated that they would keep the goods they had confiscated from the Normans to give to the rightful king upon his return.

Lady Marian admitted that she may have been hasty in her judgment, then asked Robin why he had decided to be an outlaw and live in the woods like an animal. He queried this, asking if she really wanted to know or if she was afraid of the truth or even himself, to which she retorted that she was afraid of nothing, least of all Robin.

At that point, Robin Hood took Lady Marian to see the families who had suffered and whose homes had been burned under Prince John's regency. Lady Marian softened but continued to accuse Robin of killing Normans. He admitted that he did kill those who deserved it, but that it was injustice that he despised, not the Normans.

To her credit, Lady Marian quickly began to see why Robin forsook his life of comfort and security to help the villagers and live as an outlaw. Robin kissed her hand, then told Sir Guy of Gisbourne that he should thank Lady Marian for saving his life, for it was only because of her presence that he had not been killed.

After their release, Sir Guy, Prince John, and the Sheriff of Nottingham plotted to capture Robin Hood. They decided to hold an archery contest and allowed Lady Marian to present the golden arrow to the winner. Certainly, they surmised, this would be far too tempting for Robin Hood to ignore.

Sure enough, when the day of the tournament arrived, Robin Hood appeared in disguise. He won when he split the last opponent's arrow, but as soon as Lady Marian had presented him with the golden arrow, he was overwhelmed by the guards and arrested. It was announced, much to Lady

Marian's horror, that Robin would be "hanged by the neck until dead" the following morning.

Lady Marian fretted in her tower room, but then asked Bess how she could get a message to Robin Hood's men. Bess told her there was a tavern which some of the men frequented, and Marian went forth. At the tavern, Friar Tuck had her swear "to the good lady" that she wanted to help Robin and that her coming was not another trap. Then, she revealed to him and the rest of the band that she had a plan to save the man with whom she had fallen in love.

The next day, the gallows were prepared for Robin Hood's hanging. Sir Guy of Gisbourne noticed that Lady Marian's hand was trembling, but she need not have worried. For Robin's men were all in attendance and they staged a rescue. Robin, with hands tied behind his back, hopped onto a horse—this was one of the few stunts Errol Flynn did not do himself—and rode away.

When evening fell, Robin Hood climbed the ivy up to Lady Marian's chambers, where she was sitting with Bess and speaking of her affection for him. She told Bess that Robin was different from anyone she had ever known. He was at once brave but reckless, yet at the same time, kind and gentle. She begged Bess to tell her whether when loving someone it was hard to think of anyone but that person.

As Bess confirmed that this was so, Robin startled them when he materialized from the shadows. He said that his men had told him what Lady Marian had done for him and he had come to thank her. Upon Lady Marian's pleading, Bess left them alone. Robin confessed he overheard the conversation and admitted that he was also in love with her. "Terribly," he said.

At first, Marian denied her feelings, then gave in to them. Robin called her his "bold Norman beauty" and she laughingly said, "I'm not bold." But we know that was not true, for she risked her own safety to ensure his.

Robin asked her to come with him to Sherwood Forest, noting that he had nothing to offer but a life of danger and hardship but that they would be together. He added that Friar Tuck could marry them. Marian refused to go, but only because she had come to realize that what Robin had been doing for the people of the town was right, and that the aristocracy was wrong. She wanted to join his just cause and believed she could be of much more use by staying in the castle to try and discover any further treachery. The two of them kissed and parted.

Not long afterward, Prince John received word that his brother, King Richard, had returned to the area. Lady Marian eavesdropped and heard that Prince John was planning to kill the king to secure his place on the throne. However, when she was in the middle of writing a message to warn King Richard, Sir Guy of Gisbourne discovered her deception and brought her before Prince John.

Lady Marian gave a rousing speech, in which she admitted that she did not want to believe that Normans were capable of such cruelty. But now she realized that some of them were like beasts, and got drunk on human blood. Prince John told her that she would be sorry she interfered, then ordered her execution for treason in 48 hours.

Bess told Robin's men and implored them to tell him what happened so that he could save Lady Marian. Meanwhile, King Richard, disguised as an abbot, found Robin's camp in Sherwood Forest, just as Much, the Miller's Son, arrived to tell of the plot to kill Marian. King Richard revealed who he was and Much told everyone about the danger Lady Marian was in.

King Richard, Robin, and the merry men convinced the bishop to allow them to be disguised as his monks and march to the castle. Once there, they engaged in a battle with Prince John's guards. Robin Hood fought Sir Guy of Gisbourne, killing him. Then, he forced the guard of Lady Marian's cell to open it and he rescued his lady love.

King Richard took back his throne, declaring that both Normans and Saxons should share the same rights as Englishmen. He restored Robin's rank and commanded him to take the hand of the Lady Marian in marriage. Robin very happily complied.

Like Douglas Fairbanks' film, *The Adventures of Robin Hood* was a smash hit with audiences, both domestically and overseas. It has since become a beloved classic.

Chapter Fifteen

Maid Marian Screen Depictions in the 1950s, 60s, and 70s

After these two prominent features, Maid Marian as a character did not appear in Robin Hood films again until 1952, when Walt Disney British Productions and RKO Pictures teamed up to fund *The Story of Robin Hood* (Wikipedia, 2023ai). This was Walt Disney's second feature-length, live-action film after *Treasure Island*, and like that movie, it was filmed in England. This time, British actors were in the key roles of Robin Hood and Lady Marian—Richard Todd and Joan Rice, respectively.

The motion picture was well received, especially in Britain, where it was one of the most popular of its year. An article that ran in *The New York Times* the year the movie was released claimed it to be "an expert rendition of an ancient legend that is as pretty as its Technical hues and as lively as a sturdy Western." It also described Maid Marian as "an ever-loving wench who can recognize a hero when she sees one."

The 1960 film *Sword of Sherwood Forest* starred Richard Greene in the role of Robin Hood (Wikipedia, 2023aj). Greene had previously played the part of Robin in a television series that ran from 1955 to 1959. Sarah Branch played the part of Maid Marian in the film and *The New York Times* claimed that she was "certainly the curviest Lady Marian we've ever seen." This movie was produced by British Eastmancolor.

Four years later, in 1964, a decidedly different take on the legend was released. Entitled *Robin and the 7 Hoods*, it was a musical that changed the medieval British setting to 1920s Chicago (Wikipedia, 2023s). Among its famous cast were Frank Sinatra as Robbo, Dean Martin as Little John, Sammy Davis Jr. as Will, and Bing Crosby as Allen A. Dale. The character of Marian Stevens was played by Barbara Rush, and in this film, she does not marry Robbo, but at the end of the movie is partnered with Allen A. Dale.

A return to the classic setting is found in the 1967 film *A Challenge for Robin Hood*, although the background of this film has a bit of a twist (Wikipedia, 2023d). Barrie Ingham plays Robin de Courtenay, whose cousin Roger murders his brother and blames him for the murder. As a result, Robin goes into hiding in the forest. There, he meets up with some other outlaws and is renamed Robin Hood. Lady Marian Fitzwarren is played by actress Gay Hamilton. After several exchanges involving Robin and his men and the Sheriff of Nottingham and his soldiers, Marian and her brother are captured by the sheriff and so is Robin. Robin's men save him and he in turn rescues Marian. They all return to the forest where Friar Tuck marries Robin and Marian.

Wolfshead: The Legend of Young Robin Hood is a short adventure film shot in 1969 (Wikipedia, 2024d). It was originally intended as a television pilot for a proposed TV series that never eventuated. It starred David Warbeck as Robin Hood and Ciaran Madden as an immaculate but insipid Lady Marian Fitzwalter. Her appearances in the movie were brief and did nothing for our heroine in terms of portraying her as a fearless, brave warrior fighting alongside or otherwise assisting her love, Robin Hood, in his mission against the authorities. The film was released in cinemas in 1973 as a double bill for Cliff Richard's movie *Take Me High*.

The following decade would usher in the first major animated feature depicting the legend of Robin Hood (IMDb, 2023d; Wikipedia, 2023v). It was by Disney, of course, in 1973, and their stellar animation was seen in the anthropomorphic characters who populated Sherwood Forest. Both Robin Hood and Maid Marian were red foxes, Little John was a brown bear, Friar Tuck a badger, Prince John and his brother, King Richard, were lions, and the Sheriff of Nottingham was a wolf. Maid Marian's plucky companion was a hen named Lady Kluck and Prince John's counsellor, Sir Hiss, was a snake. Monica Evans was the voice of Maid Marian. She was an English actress who also played in Neil Simon's *The Odd Couple*. Coincidentally, her co-star in that play and the movie adapted from it was Carole Shelley, who lent her voice to the character of Lady Kluck. Nancy Adams provided Lady Marian's singing voice. Brian Bedford was the voice of Robin, Roger Miller was Allan-a-Dale, Terry Thomas played Sir Hiss, and Peter Ustinov was Prince John.

Like most Disney films, it featured catchy tunes, several of which were written by Roger Miller. And there were funny scenes, such as when Robin Hood and Little John dressed up as fortune tellers and tricked Prince John and Sir Hiss. For many children, then and now, this film is their first introduction to the story and its characters. The endearing qualities of this version make it memorable.

Even though *Robin Hood* was not initially considered to be one of Disney's highly acclaimed films, it was a commercial success and became a much-loved classic. It is interesting to note that it was the first of the company's animated movies to be done "post-Walt" since he had passed away in 1966. A remake of the film was announced in 2020 to be released exclusively on Disney Plus (McNary, 2020). It would be a live-action, computer-graphic hybrid. The director is rumored to be Carlos Lopez Estrada, who directed *Raya and the Last Dragon*.

Columbia Pictures made the next movie in 1976. This one was called *Robin and Marian* and was directed by Richard Lester (Wikipedia, 2023r). Sean Connery, the first James Bond, played Robin Hood and the Lady Marian role was given to the lovely Audrey Hepburn. She had not appeared in a movie during the eight years prior to this film, so it was seen as her return to the big screen.

The film *Robin and Marian* was filmed in a variety of small villages in Navarre, Spain. Its description was: "Robin Hood, aging none too gracefully, returned exhausted from the Crusades to woo and win Maid Marian one last time." And its tagline read: "Love is the greatest adventure of all."

So far, it was the only theatrical film that depicted the murder of Robin Hood at the hands of the prioress as described by the old legend used by Roger Lancelyn Green in his book. Its original title was *The Death of Robin Hood*, but Columbia changed it in the hope of making it more marketable, as well as giving equal billing to the female lead.

The twist was that Lady Marian played the prioress and so, her deed was derived from love rather than betrayal. In fact, she finally poisoned a wounded Robin Hood and then herself in a scene reminiscent of Romeo and Juliet. When Robin Hood shot his last arrow out of the window, he declared that they both should be buried wherever it landed.

The movie received mostly positive reviews and would be the only major film that included Maid Marian until 1991.

Maid Marian Depictions in the 1990s, 2000s, and to the Present

The year to retell the tale of Robin Hood, at least when it came to motion pictures, must be 1991. That year, two movies came out depicting our greenwood hero, together with his equally important love, Maid Marian.

The first was a British movie that used the tension between the Normans and Saxons as a foundational conflict, much like *The Adventures of Robin Hood* from more than 50 years before. But there the similarities ended. Simply called *Robin Hood*, the film was directed by John Irvin and produced by Sarah

Radclyffe (Wikipedia, 2023x). Most of it was shot on location in Cheshire, England at Peckforton Castle.

The lead character was played by Patrick Bergin, most familiar, perhaps as Julia Roberts' controlling husband in *Sleeping with the Enemy*—which came out the same year. Lady Marian's role went to a young Uma Thurman, who would go on to star in *Pulp Fiction* and *Kill Bill*.

In this version, Robin was Robert Hode, a Saxon earl. The Sheriff of Nottingham character was replaced by Baron Roger Daguerre, a greedy tax collector who was initially Robert's friend. Sir Guy of Gisborne also had a name change. His characterization could be seen in Sir Miles Folcanet, a cruel, vindictive Norman knight who despised Robin Hood and lusted after Lady Marian, who was Daguerre's niece.

Our good lady was promised to Folcanet, but when Daguerre remarked, "You are the most beautiful bride England has ever seen," Lady Marian replied, "I am the most pitiful bride England has ever seen." She, of course, would rather marry Robin Hood. Her hero attacked the castle to stop her wedding to Folcanet, and Daguerre eventually reconciled with him. Unlike most other variations, King Richard did not return from the Crusades at the end of the story. Rather, Daguerre committed to treat both Normans and Saxons equally in the future.

Robin Hood was meant to have a cinematic release, but there was a problem. Another film about the legendary outlaw was due to be released at the same time. So, *Robin Hood* debuted on television, appearing on the FOX network just a month before its rival hit the movie theaters. Later, it was released in Europe, Australia, New Zealand, and Japan.

And what was this competition, you may wonder? It was *Robin Hood: Prince of Thieves*, an American film starring Kevin Costner (Wikipedia, 2023ad). Costner originally rejected the role until he heard that Kevin Reynolds, who had directed him before, was going to be the director. The two of them disagreed on whether Costner's Robin of Locksley should have an accent. Costner said he should, while Reynolds thought it may be distracting—maybe he did not want to hurt Costner's feelings by telling him his accent was not up to par. The result was a very inconsistent delivery on Costner's part. Despite criticism over his performance, though, the movie was a box office smash hit. In fact, it was the second highest-grossing film of the year, only beaten by *Terminator 2: Judgement Day*.

That may have had something to do with the rest of the cast, as well as the unique twists on the original folktale. Pen Densham, the British producer and writer, decided to make Robin Hood less of an adventurer and more of a wealthy young man who turned into a justice-seeking rebel after joining the Crusades and being imprisoned in Jerusalem. Densham gave an outline to John Watson, his fellow producer, who turned it into a screenplay that caught the attention of the production company Morgan Creek.

In this rendition, Morgan Freeman portrayed a new character to come into the story, Azeem Edin Bashir Al Bakir, a Moor whose life was saved by Robin when he broke out of prison. Azeem helped them out of Jerusalem and accompanied Robin back to England.

A youthful Christian Slater came on as a hot-headed Will Scarlett, and Alan Rickman gave a highly lauded performance as the Sheriff of Nottingham. Rickman turned down the role twice, but eventually accepted it once he was told that he could depict the character as he liked. He won a BAFTA award for his portrayal, despite some of his scenes having been edited out of the film because the studio was concerned that Rickman would steal the limelight from Costner.

Morgan Freeman was also praised for his acting skills, especially by the famous critic Roger Ebert, who claimed he was the only one to find the right tone for the film. Ebert enjoyed Rickman's depiction of the sheriff, however, he felt that it did not fit with the tone of the story. The theme song for *Robin*

Hood: Prince of Thieves was Bryan Adams' "(Everything I Do) I Do It for You," which won both an Academy Award and a Grammy.

But wait, we haven't mentioned our heroine yet. Who was Lady Marian? One Mary Elizabeth Mastrantonio, who had formerly been seen in *Scarface*, *The Color of Money*, and *The Abyss*. Of her, Roger Ebert acquiesced that she did what she could with the role, but "must have been confused when the screenplay gave her a thoughtful, independent woman in the earlier scenes, and then turned her into a clichéd damsel in distress at the end" (Ebert, 1991).

In this film, Lady Marian was the cousin of Richard the Lionheart and in this version of the legend, she had a brother, Peter Dubois. This may have been a reference to the French name of Robin Hood, *Robin des Bois*. Peter fought at Robin's side in the Third Crusade, but they were captured and spent years in an Ayyubid prison. Eventually, they escaped and saved the life of the Moor named Azeem. However, during the escape, Peter was fatally wounded.

Before he died, Peter extracted a promise from Robin that he would protect his sister Marian once he returned to England. And when Robin arrived with Azeem by his side, he discovered that his father had been killed by the sheriff's men because he had remained loyal to King Richard. This was the instigation for his avenging motivation.

There was another interesting female character in the film—Mortianna, played by Geraldine McEwan, a witch whom the Sheriff of Nottingham consulted about the future. She warned the sheriff that Robin Hood and his companion would be his undoing, and that Robin must be killed. In an extended version of the movie that was released on DVD in 2003, a previously cut scene reveals that Mortianna was the sheriff's birth mother.

But back to Lady Marian who was the object of the sheriff's desires. When Robin went to her castle to fulfill his vow, he found her handmaiden Sarah pretending to be her and he was attacked by a swordsman in black garb. Only when he disarmed the swordsman did he realize that it was not a man at all, but the true Lady Marian. She promptly gave him a swift kick in the groin before she recognized him in turn.

Lady Marian did not appear to need Robin's protection and preferred to stay and take care of the people in Nottingham as best she could. When Robin insisted upon staying, even as Guy of Gisborne and his men were ambushing them, she told the soon-to-be outlaw, "I say no more boyish gestures." Though they had spent time together as children, there was little love between them at this point. But of course, that changed over the course of the movie.

After Robin found a band of outlaws in the woods, he joined them and became their leader, encouraging them to fight back against the corrupt authorities whenever they could. Lady Marian aided his good intentions whenever the opportunity arose. Alas, Marian was taken prisoner when she tried to send King Richard a message about the sheriff's plots for Nottingham. Her betrayer was a bishop.

Mortianna convinced the sheriff to hire Celtic warriors to attack Robin Hood's camp once they found it. Many of the merry men were put in prison and the sheriff told Lady Marian that the man she had now fallen in love with was dead. He proposed to her, promising that he would spare the lives of the foresters and their children if she agreed. She unhappily consented, but the sheriff had plans to hang them all anyway during the wedding.

On the day of the ceremony, Robin and the small number of men he had left headed to Nottingham Castle with the hope of freeing the prisoners. While Azeem riled the peasants in a revolt, the sheriff hid in his keep with Lady Marian. He forced the bishop to marry them and was just about to consummate their union when Robin interrupted his wicked intentions.

He killed the sheriff after a well-choreographed fight. Then, Azeem slayed the witch Mortianna. Since he did it in defense of Robin, Azeem felt that finally his life debt had been repaid. He left the two lovers alone, and they immediately confessed their feelings for each other.

"You came for me," Marian said. "You're alive."

Robin replied, "I would die for you," before pulling her in for a kiss.

In the final scene of *Prince of Thieves*, Friar Tuck was preparing to marry Robin Hood and Lady Marian in Sherwood Forest when they were graced with a special visitor. King Richard arrived and stopped the wedding, wishing to be the one to give the bride away, which he did to the accompaniment of cheers that rang out throughout the forest.

Just two years later, a parody of the Robin Hood tale came out. Directed by Mel Brooks, who also co-wrote the screenplay with Evan Chandler and J. David Shapiro, *Robin Hood: Men in Tights* was a hilarious, musical romp that poked fun at the past retellings—especially *Robin Hood: Prince of Thieves*, upon which the plot was loosely based (IMDb, 2023b). Like that film, Brooks' iteration had Robin Hood imprisoned at the beginning. Cary Elwes was Robin of Loxley, who became an outlaw after he escaped from a prison in Jerusalem with the help of Asneeze, another inmate. Asneeze asked him to find his son, Ahchoo, in England, and Robin did just that. Ahchoo is played by Dave Chapelle, who would go on to be a master comedian after this, his first acting role in a film.

You can probably tell the kind of lighthearted, jokey tone Brooks used just by looking at their names, even if you haven't seen his other parodies like *Blazing Saddles* and *Space Balls*. The always funny Richard Lewis was a sniveling Prince John, Roger Rees was the Sheriff of Rottingham who constantly mixed up his words, and Robin's blind servant Blinkin who was meant to be a representation of the servant Duncan in *Prince of Thieves*, was played by Mark Blankfield. Brooks' regular Dom DeLuise had a brief role as Don Giovanni, a mafioso character whom the sheriff hired to assassinate Robin.

Amy Yasbeck, who had supporting roles in *The Mask* and *Pretty Woman*, is the redheaded Lady Marian, who wore an Everlast chastity belt. Lamenting how long she has waited for true love, she also includes innuendo about the right man having the key to her chastity belt. Lady Marian even had her own solo song with Debbie James providing her singing voice.

Even through the comedy, the romantic heart that had always been a part of the folktale was never lost. And the laughs also never stopped in this comedy adventure, where the merry men sang about their tight tights and Prince John's mole moved around his face from scene to scene. It had a very different tone but there were totally recognizable plot points from the films that came before it, and it also had an influence on the films that followed.

Now let us jump forward eight more years to 2001, when Disney decided to revisit the legendary characters again, or their daughter, rather. They released a live-action TV movie *Princess of Thieves* during *The Wonderful World of Disney* segment on ABC (IMDb, 2023c; Wikipedia, 2023p).

Kiera Knightley of *Love Actually*, *Pirates of the Caribbean*, *Pride and Prejudice* and *Black Doves* fame, to mention a few, played the hero and heroine's strong-willed daughter, Gwyn. Her mother had died, and Robin Hood was away fighting in the Crusades. When King Richard the Lionheart also died, Robin returned to England and was taken by his enemies, the Sheriff of Nottingham and Prince John. Now, it was up to Gwyn to rescue him.

A twist to the tale is a young character, Prince Philip, who had returned from exile in France to claim the throne and was traveling *incognito*. Of course, Marian's and Philip's paths crossed, and a romantic spark hovered between them. Together with the merry men, they freed Robin and then stopped the coronation of Prince John. Just before Philip was to be crowned king, Gwyn told him that they could not be a couple, and she could only serve him as her monarch. In the final scenes, Gwyn and Robin were seen leading the merry men together.

In 2009, *Beyond Sherwood Forest* aired as a movie made for television (IMDb, 2023a). It had an interesting twist—a huge dragon. Actually—spoiler alert—it was a shapeshifting young woman. The Sheriff of Nottingham sent the dragon into Sherwood Forest to kill Robin Hood. Meanwhile, Marian had fled to the safety of the greenwood to escape an arranged marriage with an Austrian prince. This television movie was action-packed with different twists to the well-known tale, such as the dragon.

One noticeable blunder is that many scenes in the Sherwood Forest of the movie are set in what is largely a coniferous forest, unlike the real English forest which is largely composed of deciduous trees. Originally a vestige of an older Royal Hunting Forest, Sherwood today is a mixture of low shrub, woodland, heath, and pasture (Edwinstowe Historical Society, 2023). However, in the period 1154 to 1485, the forest was renowned for being so thickly overgrown, with the intermingling of trees and branches, that any paths were difficult to follow. It would have been an ideal area for outlaws to wander unseen and hide.

The next year takes us to Ridley Scott's 2010 version, *Robin Hood* with Russell Crowe as Robin and Cate Blanchett in the title roles (Wikipedia, 2023z). Here, other writers were inspired to put a bit of a twist on the classic. They focused more on the origin of the hero. For the plot of this film, Crowe's character was called Robin Longstride, and he was a veteran archer from the Crusades who deserted the battle once King Richard was dead. Cate Blanchett played Marion Loxley, a widow.

On his way back to England, he promised a severely wounded knight named Sir Robert Loxley that he would go to Nottingham and return Loxley's sword to his father. But when he got back to England, Robin Longstride had to assume Loxley's identity so that he could tell the royal family about the death of King Richard. As Loxley, he witnessed the coronation of the next in line: King John played by Oscar Isaac. As in most of the other variations, King John immediately ordered taxes to be raised.

When Robin reached Nottingham, he found Loxley's blind father, Sir Walter, who asked him to continue with the impersonation of his son so that the lands and estate of the family did not get seized by King John.

Robin also met Loxley's widow, Marion. She was initially distrustful of Robin Longstride but started to warm to him a little once he and his companions gave the townspeople grain to plant. It was a good thing, because they had to share a chamber to pull off the ruse that Robin was her husband. He gained more renown as he led the northern barons in battle, but he could not prevent French marauders, led by the wicked Godfrey, from killing Sir Walter Loxley. Robin then led the English army, now united thanks to his help, in battle against the French.

At one point, Godfrey tried to slay Marion but Robin killed him with a well-shot arrow. The French realized that they would not be able to divide England so ceased their plans to invade. You would think this would have pleased King John, but he was more concerned about Robin Longstride being a threat to his power. So, he declared Robin to be an outlaw.

By now, Robin and Marion had become inseparable, and they fled, together with a band of men and orphans, into Sherwood Forest. As the narrator at the end, Marion told us:

> "The greenwood is the outlaws' friend. Now, the orphan boys make us welcome. No tax, no tithe, nobody rich, nobody poor . . ."

Then the last bit of text reads:

> "And so the legend begins."

Ridley Scott's *Robin Hood* received mixed reviews; however, it was far better received than the next retelling made in 2018. Also titled *Robin Hood*, this was supposed to be somewhat of a contemporary version of the tale (Wikipedia, 2023aa). The cast seemed to have more modern-looking clothing and haircuts, but the story was still meant to be set in medieval England although there were many historical inaccuracies.

Directed by Otto Bathurst, the film starred Taron Egerton, best known for his lead roles in *Rocketman* and *Kingsman*. Jamie Foxx, the Arabian warrior Yahya—which apparently can be translated to John—acted as his mentor. Most accounts claim that this character was poorly written. The talented Foxx, who won an Academy Award for Best Actor for his portrayal of Ray Charles in 2004, as well as numerous other awards, was even nominated for a Razzie which is a parody award given to the worst achievements in films, for Worst Supporting Actor. Besides Foxx's Razzie nomination, it was also nominated for Worst Picture and Worst Remake.

In her debut in a big-budget feature, Eve Hewson, the daughter of Bono from the band U2, played Maid Marian. Her acting was praised for the most part, with many people predicting her success in the future, despite her involvement with this unsuccessful movie. In a *Variety* review, Hewson was described as having "the stuff to be a major movie star . . . as a supremely sensual and spirited Marian who takes her commands from no man" (Gleiberman, 2018). While her independence was well-documented, even in some of the oldest variations, this depiction of the heroine had also been criticized for showing so much cleavage it would have been seen as scandalous in the Middle Ages.

The storyline surrounds Robin of Loxley, an aristocrat called to fight in the Crusades, returning home after four years away to find his lands seized and his former lover, Marian, in the arms of his former friend, Will. So, he has the rest of the film to build himself back up and become a freedom fighter.

Unfortunately, it was not only a critical flop, but a financial one as well. The production budget was $100 million, but the film only grossed $86 million. Michael O'Sullivan, in a review for the Washington Post, called *Robin Hood* "a chilly and flavorless frappé of historical speculation, revisionist folklore, and every lazy action-movie cliché ever written" (O'Sullivan, 2018). Most other critics agreed, and a planned sequel will probably never see the light of day. Hopefully, this is a lesson for any future film creators inspired by the medieval saga.

There is a recent film where Marian is the main character: *The Adventures of Maid Marian*, starring Sophie Craig (The Guardian, 2023). In this made-for-television movie, Marian learns that King Richard is dead. Robin Hood returns from the holy wars, only to be badly wounded by the Sheriff of Nottingham. It is up to Marian to keep him alive as they hide deep in the forest and fight off the mercenaries sent to kill him. Unfortunately, this offering was not well received. The Guardian described it as "almost comically unmedieval" and falling flat probably because of resources that were stretched too thinly.

Besides the live-action Disney version to be released on their streaming channel, there have been several rumors circulating that multiple production companies have Robin Hood films in the works.

There was an announcement in 2017 for a film about Marian that would star Margot Robbie as the heroine (Kroll, 2017). Margot has starred in many headlining movies, the latest being *Barbie*. The story for this, aptly titled *Marian*, would focus on the war waged by Maid Marian after the death of her beloved Robin Hood. The script was written by Pete Barry and is still considered to be in production, so hopefully it will grace the big screen sometime soon.

Meanwhile, it has also been reported that Hugh Jackman (*Les Misérables*) and Jodie Comer (*Killing Eve*) are due to star in a new movie to be called *The Death of Robin Hood* (Wiseman, 2024). The movie will be a darker version of the traditional Robin Hood story. Set in the present era, it will follow the eponymous character as he struggles with his past following a life of crime and murder. As a battle-weary recluse who is seriously hurt, he is cared for by an enigmatic woman who gives him hope for redemption. Production is planned for early 2025.

It is time for the legend's female lead to take center stage and such a contemporary retelling would be compelling. For now, let us stay with the small screen of television, where Robin Hood productions have been numerous, and several intriguing iterations of Maid Marian show her further development over the years.

Chapter Sixteen

Maid Marian on Television

The first TV show depicting a version of the legend was the BBC's *Robin Hood*, which was a series of six episodes that aired in 1953 (Wikipedia, 2023u). The forest outlaw was played by Patrick Troughton and Maid Marian, who only appeared in the final episode, *The Secret*, was portrayed by Josée Richard. Much more well-known is the series that came out two years later and lasted for 143 episodes: *The Adventures of Robin Hood* (Wikipedia, 2023c).

In this version, which was played on TV channels across the world, the character of Lady Marian Fitzwater was a Norman-Irish noblewoman who was just as skilled an archer as Robin Hood. In the first two seasons of the series, Bernadette O'Farrell played her, while Patricia Driscoll took over for the last two series. Richard Greene was the aptly named actor who played the lead role of Robin Hood.

Even though the series was rife with historical errors and anachronisms, it was a success. An interesting bit of trivia surrounding *The Adventures of Robin Hood* is that its producer, Hannah Weinstein, brought on several blacklisted writers to pen their scripts under pseudonyms. At the time, these writers were suspected of having Communist leanings, so they were denied work in Hollywood.

As a character, Maid Marian did not reappear in a major television depiction until 1984. *Robin of Sherwood* premiered that year, and was a mix of grim history, fiction, and pagan mythology (Wikipedia, 2023ae). This series is considered to be one of the most influential treatments of the core Robin Hood legend since the classic film *The Adventures of Robin Hood*. It featured a realistic period setting and Creator Richard Carpenter added elements of fantasy to the story, which had not featured in previous televised versions of the tale. These included Robin's supernatural mentor, Herne the Hunter, his magic sword Albion and various appearances by black magicians and demons. The historian Stephen Knight lauded it as "the most innovative and influential version of the myth in recent times."

Michael Praed was the first Robin Hood character, Robin of Loxley, but he was killed at the end of the second season by Norman crossbowmen. Meanwhile, Judi Trott was the red-haired Saxon noblewoman Lady Marion of Leaford. She escaped the clutches of the evil Baron Simon de Belleme, played by Anthony Valentine. The nobleman was a devil worshipper who claimed he wanted Marion as his bride but was really intending to use her as a sacrifice to his demons. Robin rescued her from the Baron de Belleme and she escaped with him to Sherwood Forest. They fell in love and were married, and she lived with Robin and the merry men in the forest and bravely took part in many of their escapades. She was heartbroken when Robin died. Following his death, Jason Connery, the son of another Robin Hood iteration in film, Sean Connery, played Robert of Huntingdon who was chosen by Herne to take up the mantle of Robin Hood and become the new leader of the outlaws. He rescued Marion from another unwanted marriage and went on to court her.

Other protagonists included Robert de Rainault, Sheriff of Nottingham, portrayed by Nickolas Grace. He was the king's chief representative in Nottingham and neighbouring Sherwood. Sir Guy of Gisburne was played by Robert Addie. Sir Guy was the Steward of the Abbot's lands and was the chief military commander in the district. The Abbot of St Mary's, Hugo de

Rainault, was the highest-ranking churchman in Nottingham. Played by Philip Jackson, he was the younger brother of the Sheriff and was more interested in acquiring land than concerning himself with church matters.

Robin's merry men included Much (Peter Llewellyn Williams), Will Scarlet (Ray Winstone), Little John of Hathersage (Clive Mantle) and Friar Tuck (Phil Rose). Nasir, a Saracen outlaw played by Mark Ryan, had been captured in Palestine by Baron de Belleme. The Baron had forced him to return to England and work for him. Robin killed the Baron then afterward in a momentous sword fight, Nasir found respect for Robin and decided to join his band of men. His archery skills matched Robin's and he fought with double swords and had exceptional tracking abilities.

Herne the Hunter, played by John Abineri, was a shamanic figure who often incarnated a forest spirit. He appeared wearing a stag's head and antlers and represented the powers of goodness and light. He protected Robin, the Hooded Man, from hazardous situations as well as inspiring and guiding him. According to Carpenter, he was based on the Pagan principle of the Horned god.

In 1989, our heroine, played by Kate Lonergan, got her name in the title of a show, *Maid Marian And Her Merry Men* (Robinson, 2023). This was a children's musical comedy show written by Sir Tony Robinson but enjoyed by people of all ages It lasted four seasons and was centered on the premise that Maid Marian was the true leader of the Sherwood Forest outlaws while Robin Hood was completely incompetent. However, Marian was not recognized as the leader outside the group.

Many children's series made by the British have social commentary and witty satire in them, and this show was no exception. Not only was the royal family referenced, along with other cultural themes, but there were also nods to previous incarnations of the Robin Hood legend. Because of the show's success, an adaptation was created for the stage as well as a cartoon strip written by Paul Cemmick that appeared in the *Daily Telegraph's* children's paper, *The Young Telegraph*.

In 2018, Sir Tony disclosed plans for a stage show and further talks about bringing the show back also took place in 2021 and 2022. Sir Tony stated in 2023 that he had sold the rights to *Maid Marian And Her Merry Men* to a production company and he was working with that company to produce a version for television (Goodall, 2023). A theatrical adaptation of the 1990s television series was also scheduled to debut in 2024 (British Comedy Guide, 2024). Sir Tony is reportedly collaborating with musical comedian Vikki Stone on the project's script. In preparation for a UK premiere late in 2024, a workshop for *Maid Marian And Her Merry Men: A New Musical* (*sort of)* was scheduled for January 25, 2024, at London's Soho Theatre. It was announced that Vikki Stone, would play the Sheriff of Nottingham in this new musical version. She wrote the book, the music, and the lyrics. Bronté Barbé was apparently cast as Maid Marian in the workshop but no further information has been released.

When the 1990s arrived, there was a slew of television shows about heroes, such as *Hercules: The Legendary Journeys* and *Xena: Warrior Princess*. Similar in tone and style to these memorable shows was *The New Adventures of Robin Hood*, which premiered in 1997 on TNT and ran for four seasons (Wikipedia, 2023l).

Matthew Porretta was the archer outlaw to start with, and interestingly, he had portrayed Will Scarlett O'Hara in the *Robin Hood: Men in Tights* movie just a handful of years prior to this. John Bradley took over for him in the last half of the series. The first season had Anna Galvin as Lady Marion Fitzwalter while Barbara Griffin played her for the rest of the run. In one episode, Marion saves her young cousin from her corrupt sister-in-law, who kidnaps the girl to give her to an evil noble as his bride. In another, Marion is the one who is kidnapped by a wicked cult leader who wants to make her the bride of his dark god.

This show incorporated quite a lot of fantastical elements, including monsters, enchanted weapons, and even time travel. It added a new character into the legend, too—Olwyn the wizard who was played by Christopher Lee. Olwyn's character was a mentor to Robin Hood.

The BBC aired another version of the folktale in 2006 (Wikipedia, 2023y). Simply titled *Robin Hood*, it went back to traditional roots, having Robin Hood return home from the Crusades to find the Sheriff of Nottingham using his authority to intimidate and frighten the peasants and bleed them dry. Robin was outlawed. He set up camp in Sherwood Forest with several allies and began his outlaw activities from his camp.

Foz Allen, co-creator with Dominic Minghella of *Doc Martin* fame, toured England, Ireland and Europe looking for the right location that would have studio space and interesting woodlands. Finally, the series was shot in Hungary with most of the houses and the castle interior specially constructed for the show. At the start of production, there was a rigorous training process for the cast who needed to be proficient in unarmed combat, the use of bows and arrows and different types of swords and of course, horse-riding stunts (Moreland, 2021).

In August 2006, four tapes of footage were stolen from the studio in Hungary (BBC News, 2006). This resulted in the disruption of schedules as well as missed production deadlines. At the time, there was a rumor that a ransom was paid to secure the return of the tapes. Eventually, local police found them in September.

In this series, Jonas Armstrong played a more subtle Robin Hood than the gung-ho character often portrayed by other actors who have taken the part. Lucy Griffiths was a beautiful, independent and feisty Maid Marian whose face seemed somewhat over-rouged. Richard Armitage, as a brooding Sir Guy of Gisborne, was an excellent foil for Keith Allen's interpretation of the mocking and sarcastic Vaisey, Sheriff of Nottingham. Sam Troughton, grandson of Patrick Troughton who had played Robin in the 1953 BBC series, took the part of Robin's best friend Much who spent a great deal of time thinking about food, sometimes at the most inappropriate moments in the plot.

Robin and Marian were in a love triangle with the third member being Sir Guy of Gisborne. Sir Guy killed Lady Marian in the second series, as she was attempting to protect the wounded King Richard. As she lay dying, Robin Hood and Lady Marian were married.

The third season brought a new love interest for the archer, Isabella, who was Sir Guy's sister. Played by Lara Pulver, Isabella had a secret relationship with Robin Hood, but she desired power even more and eventually became a ruthless and corrupt sheriff. During the third season, many actors including Jonas Armstrong, left. As a result, the BBC canceled the show.

The fantasy-adventure show *Once Upon a Time*, on television from 2011 to 2018, had many characters from fairy tales and folktales (Wikipedia, 2023m). Christie Laing played the role of Maid Marian in one episode in the fifth season, where she ran away from the Sheriff of Nottingham after falling in love with Robin Hood. She fell ill shortly after becoming pregnant and Robin Hood had to go into Rumplestiltskin's castle to get a magic wand to heal her.

When Rumpelstiltskin wanted to kill Robin because of his theft, his maid Belle begged him not to so that Robin's child with Marian would not grow up fatherless. Rumpelstiltskin fired a warning shot, and they escaped into the woods.

Doctor Who also brought Lady Marian in as a character in their episode, "Robot of Sherwood" (Wikipedia, 2023af). The Twelfth Doctor had to save her from the dungeon guarded by the sheriff, before he even knew who she, or Robin Hood, was—or even that they were real.

Of course, as we have seen with films, animation is also a great medium to portray the legend. Both hand-drawn and 3D animated adaptations of the Robin Hood tale have been created and of course, feature Maid Marian.

Animated Series Featuring Maid Marian

An animation studio in Canada created a unique show titled *Rocket Robin Hood* that set the familiar characters in space in the year 3000 and living on the New Sherwood Forest Asteroid (Wikipedia, 2023ag). Running from 1966 to 1969, one of the top animators was Jean Mathieson, a Canadian who was among the first women in the industry.

Robin Fuddo no Daibōken, translated to *"Robin Hood's Great Adventure,"* an Italian-Japanese cartoon series, came out in 1990 with another twist (Wikipedia, 2023w). This featured pre-teens as the characters of Robin Hood and his friends. There were fifty-two episodes made, all in the classic animated style, and Robin had some new allies in his girl cousins Winifred and Jenny, who were sisters to Will Scarlet.

The character of Marian Lancaster in this series is interesting. She hailed from the noble Lancaster family and wore a golden cross around her neck which belonged to her mother and was a symbol of her family. Throughout the series, Marian's character developed and evolved, and she was more fleshed out than the other characters. Marian was voiced by Naoko Matsui in the Japanese version. This also had her being chased by a greedy older man, Bishop Hartford, who, in the Japanese version of the show, wanted to marry her to obtain her family's estate. However, in the English adaptation, Bishop Hartford wanted to adopt Marian, whose English voice is provided by Katherine Shannon.

The following year saw Hanna-Barbera release an animated version of the legend which also made the characters younger than their previous counterparts. Their show was called *Young Robin Hood* and ran for two seasons during *The Funtastic World of Hanna-Barbera* on Sunday mornings (Wikipedia, 2023al).

A teenage Robin Hood escapes the clutches of the Sheriff of Nottingham by heading into Sherwood Forest while his father, the Earl of Huntingdon, was away fighting in the Crusades with King Richard. There, he was joined by other young rebels. Marian, voiced by Anik Matern, was the sheriff's ward, though she acted as a spy for Robin Hood. The sheriff's lieutenant, Gilbert of Gisbourn, had a crush on Marian and while trying to win her affections, often spilt information to her. There was a witch in this funny iteration of the tale named Haggala. But she was kind-hearted instead of cruel, and her spells did not always work.

The legendary tale got the computer-generated treatment in *Robin Hood: Mischief in Sherwood* in 2016 (Wikipedia, 2023ac). This show originally aired as fifteen-minute segments, but these have sometimes been paired up so that the episodes were longer. Again, Robin Hood was a teenager, this time voiced by Tom Wayland, and Maid Marian was voiced by Sarah Natochenny. In Season Three, Robin's brother Rowan Hood and Marian's sister Maria were introduced. The younger siblings had crushes on each other, just like Robin Hood and Marian.

So many other television shows have had the familiar figures appear. In 1970, Lynn Redgrave guest starred on *The Muppet Show* as Maid Marian. Of course, Kermit the Frog was Robin Hood during the episode. And there have been many more iterations beyond that.

When the number of times the legend has been transformed for page, theater, or movie is considered, it is a marvelous testament to its enduring quality.

Chapter Seventeen - Conclusion

Whether in a film or show, on the stage or during the May Games, sung about in taverns, or gracing the pages of classic literature, no one can deny that Maid Marian has a longstanding and highly acclaimed presence in folklore. The early ballads and plays may have brought about her materialization, but it took all the writers and actresses who came afterward who cemented her so firmly in the imaginations of people across the globe.

She is truly one of the most referenced female figures in the whole Western canon and Robin Hood just would not be the same without her. Yet, as we've seen, Maid Marian does not need Robin for her to be a well-rounded and capable woman in her own right. After all, she was a character all by herself before she was linked up with him.

This does not mean, though, that the love portrayed by them in all the various iterations of their story is not something truly special. For whether the Robin Hood figure is depicted as playful and fun-loving, vengeful and ruthless, or dark and brooding, he always treats his lady, Marian, with great respect and admiration in any of the versions in which she makes an appearance. And the merry men hail her as their queen, at least inside Sherwood Forest.

Just from this, we can see that her character commands a level of reverence that may be in large part due to her shows of strength, bravery, and independence. And it is these traits that define womanhood, not only for the fictional figure of Maid Marian, but for all women the world over. They deserve to be appreciated and upheld with dignity, and if men truly want to be as heroically noble as a hero like Robin Hood, they would do well to treat women as he treats the Lady Marian.

In her own right, she loves fiercely and loyally, never breaking her vow to the man she loves, and, also, just as important, never breaking the vow she makes to herself. Her core characteristics almost always stay the same, no matter how much she has evolved over the last thousand years. That is why she has been so appealing to storytellers and no doubt will continue to be. We can only dream what future interpretations of her will look like—outlaw's sweetheart, the Lady of the Forest, the Queen of May, the beautiful Lady Marian—whose beauty and grace go far deeper than her skin.

Bibliography

Abrahams, P. (2013). *The Outlaws of Sherwood Street: Stealing from the Rich. Book 1 in the Outlaws of Sherwood Street Series*. Puffin Books.

Alchetron. (2022). *Robert Fitzwalter*. Retrieved May 13, 2023 from https://alchetron.com/Robert-Fitzwalter

Aldine Robin Hood Library. (1901-1906). *Aldine Robin Hood Library - Collected stories*. Aldine Publishing Company. Retrieved June 8, 2023 from https://digital.library.villanova.edu/Item/vudl:294849

Alfred Lord Tennyson. (n.d.). *The Foresters: Robin Hood and Maid Marian [1892]*. Retrieved June 8, 2023 from https://d.lib.rochester.edu/robin-hood/text/tennyson-foresters

Anonymous. (1700, January 6, 2021). *A Famous Battle between Robin Hood and Maid Marian*. Retrieved May 22, 2023 from https://en.wikisource.org/wiki/A_famous_battle_between_Robin_Hood,_and_Maid_Marian

Anonymous. (1819). *Robin Hood: a Tale of the Olden Time; VOL. I* Gale ECCO, Print Editions. (Oliver & Boyd, G. & W. B. Whittaker and W. Turnbull, London)

Anonymous. (2021). *George-a-Green, The Pinner of Wakefield [1599]*. Retrieved June 8, 2023 from http://elizabethandrama.org/wp-content/uploads/2021/07/George-a-Green-Annotated.pdf

Anonymous. (2025). *caput gerat lupinum*. Retrieved January 12, 2025 from https://www.lsd.law/define/caput-gerat-lupinum

Atlas Obscura. (2020, 13 October 2020). *The Tomb of Maid Marian*. Retrieved May 13, 2023 from https://www.atlasobscura.com/places/the-tomb-of-maid-marian

Basdeo, S. (2016, 20 May 2016). *Maid Marian in Victorian Penny Dreadfuls: A Proto-Feminist? A paper read at the Women in Print Conference, Chetham's Library, Manchester 20 May 2016*. Retrieved June 8, 2023 from https://reynolds-news.com/2016/05/20/maid-marian-in-victorian-penny-dreadfuls-a-proto-feminist/

BBC News. (2006, 28 August 2006). *Tapes for BBC's Robin Hood stolen*. Retrieved December 19, 2024 from http://news.bbc.co.uk/2/hi/uk_news/5292348.stm

Blanchard, A. E. (2019). *Little Maid Marian*. Publisher : Alpha Editions.

Boulton, M. T. (2019). *The Outlaws of Nottingham: The Warriors of Sherwood. Book I.* Lulu.com.

Braveheart Wiki. (2023). *Murron MacClannough* Retrieved May 9, 2023 from https://braveheart.fandom.com/wiki/Murron_MacClannough

Brewer, E. C. (1993). *The Dictionary of Phrase and Fable: Maid Marian, p. 795* [Reference]. Wordsworth Editions Ltd. (1894)

Britannica, T. E. o. E. (2007, 4 August 2023). *Anthony Munday: English poet, dramatist, pamphleteer, and translator.* Retrieved August 8, 2023 from https://www.britannica.com/biography/Anthony-Munday

Britannica, T. E. o. E. (2020, 5 May 2023). *John Henry, folk hero.* Retrieved June 1, 2023 from https://www.britannica.com/topic/John-Henry-folk-hero

Britannica, T. E. o. E. (2024a, 7 February 2024). *Adam de La Halle - The Play of Robin and Marion 1283.* Retrieved June 20, 2024 from https://www.britannica.com/biography/Adam-de-la-Halle

Britannica, T. E. o. E. (2024b, 01 November 2024). *Geoffrey Chaucer: The Canterbury Tales - 1392.* Retrieved May 8, 2023 from https://www.britannica.com/topic/The-Canterbury-Tales

British Comedy Guide. (2024, 8 January 2024). *Maid Marian And Her Merry Men stage show confirmed.* Retrieved July 21, 2024 from https://www.comedy.co.uk/live/news/7712/maid-marian-2024-stage-show-musical/

Brooke, C. K. (2019). *Marian, Princess Thief: A Robin Hood Retelling: 1.* Independently Published.

Brooke, F. (1789). *Airs, songs, chorusses [sic], &c, in Marian, a comic opera. in two acts. Performed at the Theatre-Royal, Covent-Garden. The musick by Mr. Shields [sic].* (Third ed.) [Reprinted old book]. ECCO Print Editions. (T. Cadell 1789)

Brooke, F. (1800). *Marian: a comic opera, in two acts. Performed at the Theatre-Royal, Covent-Garden. By Mrs. Brookes.* T. N. Longman and O. Rees. Retrieved June 12, 2024 from https://quod.lib.umich.edu/cgi/t/text/text-idx?c=ecco;idno=004870301.0001.000

Campbell, C. M., & Campbell, N. (c 1938). *Maid Marian.* Retrieved June 12, 2024 from http://operascotland.org/opera/653/Maid+Marian

Chase, N. (1984). *Locksley.* Penguin.

Child, F. J. (1888a). *The English and Scottish Popular Ballads Volume III. No. 117 - A Gest of Robyn Hode* (Vol. III). The Gutenberg Project. https://www.gutenberg.org/cache/epub/62474/pg62474-images.html#c117 (Houghton, Mifflin and Company)

Child, F. J. (1888b). *The English and Scottish Popular Ballads Volume III. No. 118 - Robin Hood and Guy of Gisborne* (Vol. III). The Gutenberg Project. https://www.gutenberg.org/cache/epub/62474/pg62474-images.html#c118 (Houghton, Mifflin and Company)

Child, F. J. (1888c). *The English and Scottish Popular Ballads Volume III. No. 119 - Robin Hood and the Monk* (Vol. III). The Gutenberg Project. https://www.gutenberg.org/cache/epub/62474/pg62474-images.html#c119 (Houghton, Mifflin and Company)

Child, F. J. (1888d). *The English and Scottish Popular Ballads Volume III. No. 149 - Robin Hood's Birth, Breeding, Valor and Marriage* (Vol. III). The Gutenberg Project. https://www.gutenberg.org/cache/epub/62474/pg62474-images.html#c149 (Houghton, Mifflin and Company)

Child, F. J. (1888e). *The English and Scottish Popular Ballads Volume III. No. 150 - Robin Hood and Maid Marian* (Vol. III). The Gutenberg Project. https://www.gutenberg.org/cache/epub/62474/pg62474-images.html#c150 (Houghton, Mifflin and Company)

Chu, J. (n.d.). *The history of May Day*. Retrieved May 8, 2023 from https://www.nationaltrust.org.uk/discover/history/the-history-of-may-day

Collins Dictionary. (2023). *Definition of 'pastourelle'*. Retrieved May 9, 2023 from https://www.collinsdictionary.com/dictionary/english/pastourelle

Creswick, P. (2016). *Robin Hood*. CreateSpace Independent Publishing Platform. https://www.amazon.com.au/Robin-Hood-Paul-Creswick/dp/1540627799/ref=tmm_pap_swatch_0?_encoding=UTF8&qid=&sr=

Davenport, R. (2011). *King John and Matilda, a tragedy. As it was acted with great applause by her Majesties servants at the Cock-pit in Drury-lane. 1655*. British Library, Historical Print Editions.

Davies, D. S. (2018). *David Stuart Davies looks at Robin Hood*. Retrieved March 1, 2024 from https://wordsworth-editions.com/robin-hood/

De Koven, R. (2004). *Robin Hood*. Albany Records. Retrieved August 6, 2024 from https://www.albanyrecords.com/catalog/troy0712-13/

Dobson, R. B., & Taylor, J. (1989a). Appendix IV - A Select List of Robin Hood Place Names. In *Rymes of Robyn Hood - An Introduction to the English Outlaw* (pp. 293-311). Alan Sutton Publishing. (1976)

Dobson, R. B., & Taylor, J. (1989b). Extracts from 'The Sad Shepherd' (Ben Jonson). In *Rymes of Robyn Hood - An Introduction to the English Outlaw* (pp. 231-236). Alan Sutton Publishing. (1976)

Dobson, R. B., & Taylor, J. (1989c). The Play of 'Robin Hood and the Friar', c. 1560. In *Rymes of Robyn Hood - An Introduction to the English Outlaw* (pp. 208-214). Alan Sutton Publishing. (1976)

Dobson, R. B., & Taylor, J. (1989d). The Play of 'Robin Hood and the Potter', c. 1560 In *Rymes of Robyn Hood - An Introduction to the English Outlaw* (pp. 215-219). Alan Sutton Publishing. (1976)

Dobson, R. B., & Taylor, J. (1989e). The Play of 'Robin Hood and the Sheriff', c. 1475. In *Rymes of Robyn Hood - An Introduction to the English Outlaw* (pp. 203-207). Alan Sutton Publishing. (1976)

Donald, A. (2011). *Outlaw: A Novel of Robin Hood: 1. Meet the Godfather of Sherwood Forest*. St Martin's Press.

Drayton, M. (2010). *Matilda The faire and chaste daughter of the Lord Robert Fitzwater. The true glorie of the noble house of Sussex. Originally published in 1594*. EEBO Editions, ProQuest. http://name.umdl.umich.edu/A20826.0001.001 (At London: Printed by Iames Roberts, 1594)

Dumas, A. t. b. A. R. A. (2021). *The Prince of Thieves and Robin Hood the Outlaw: Omnibus Edition, first published 1872-3* (A. Jones, Ed.)

Ebert, R. (1991, 14 June 1991). *Review: Robin Hood: Prince Of Thieves*. Retrieved July 21, 2023 from https://www.rogerebert.com/reviews/robin-hood-prince-of-thieves-1991

Edwinstowe Historical Society. (2023). *Trees of Sherwood Forest & Major Oak*. Retrieved July 23, 2023 from https://edwinstowehistory.org.uk/local-history/sherwood-forest/trees-sherwood-forest/

Egan, P. (2010). *Robin Hood and Little John; or, the Merrie Men of Sherwood Forest* (1840)

Emmett, G. (2005). *Robin Hood and the Outlaws of Sherwood Forest, [First published c. 1869]*. Routledge; 1st edition. (1885)

Feyrer, G. (1996). *The Thief's Mistress*. Dell https://www.amazon.com/Thiefs-Mistress-Gayle-Feyrer/dp/0440217784

Fortunaso, R. (1641). *Extracts from The Sad Shepherd [1641]*. Retrieved October 19, 2023 from https://robinhoodlegend.com/the-sad-shepherd/

Fortunaso, R. (n.d.-a). *Operas, Musicals, and Pantomime 2*. Retrieved October 10, 2023 from https://robinhoodlegend.com/operas-musicals-pantomime-2/

Fortunaso, R. (n.d.-b). *Robin Hood - Plays and the May Festivities*. Retrieved October 10, 2023 from https://robinhoodlegend.com/plays-festivities/

Gale, C. (2014). *Bound by Honor: An Erotic Novel of the Robin Hood Legend* (Reprint ed.). Avid Press, LLC. (2009)

Gleiberman, O. (2018, 20 November 2018). *Film Review: 'Robin Hood'*. Retrieved June 17, 2023 from https://variety.com/2018/film/reviews/robin-hood-review-taron-egerton-jamie-foxx-1203033148/#

Godwin, P. (1991). *Sherwood*. William Morrow & Co.

Godwin, P. (1993). *Robin and the King*. William Morrow & Co.

Good Reads. (2023,). *Quote from "Celestial Harmonies" by Péter Esterházy*. . Retrieved October 14, 2023 from https://www.goodreads.com/search?q=Péter+Esterházy&search%5Bsource%5D=goodreads&search_type=quotes&tab=quotes

Goodall, S. (2023, 01 May 2023). Iconic 90s BBC kids show created by Sir Tony Robinson is set to return to screens. *The Mirror*. https://www.mirror.co.uk/tv/tv-news/iconic-90s-bbc-kids-show-29855513

Gower, J. (1992). *Mirour de L'omme: [The Mirror of Mankind]*. Michigan State University Press.

Greek Mythology. (n.d.). *The myth of Pandora's box*. Retrieved May 8, 2023 from https://www.greekmyths-greekmythology.com/pandoras-box-myth/#google_vignette

Green, R. L. (2010). *The Adventures of Robin Hood*. (1956)

Green, R. L. (2016b). *The Adventures of Robin Hood*. www.greenpenguin.co.uk (1956)

Hall, E. (1809). *Hall's Chronicle; containing THE HISTORY OF ENGLAND during THE REIGN OF HENRY THE FOURTH to the end of THE REIGN OF HENRY THE EIGHTH, in which are particularly described the manners and customs of those periods, carefully collated with the editions of 1548 and 1550* (Original from the University of Michigan ed.) [Google Digitized Book]. J.JOHNSON, F.C. and J. RIVINGTON, T.PAYNE, WILDIE and ROBINSON; LONGMAN, HURST, REES and ORME; CADELL AND DAVIES; AND J.MAWMAN. https://babel.hathitrust.org/cgi/pt?id=mdp.49015000231820&view=1up&seq=525 (1809)

Heal, E. (1928). *Robin Hood*. Rand, McNally & Co. .

Historiska. (2023). *Odin – the one-eyed All-Father*. Retrieved May 8, 2023 from https://historiska.se/norse-mythology/odin-en/#:~:text=Odin%20has%20many%20names%20and,Frigg%20and%20Thor%20by%20Jord

Holocaust Encyclopedia. (n.d.). *September 29, 1938 - Munich Agreement*. Retrieved June 18, 2024 from https://encyclopedia.ushmm.org/content/en/timeline-event/holocaust/1933-1938/munich-agreement

IMDb. (2023a). *Beyond Sherwood Forest [TV movie 2009]*. Retrieved June 20, 2023 from https://www.imdb.com/title/tt1331323/

IMDb. (2023b, 10 January 2023). *Men in Tights [1993 film]*. Retrieved July 10, 2023 from https://www.imdb.com/title/tt0107977/

IMDb. (2023c). *Princess of Thieves [2001]*. Retrieved July 20, 2023 from https://www.imdb.com/title/tt0272790/

IMDb. (2023d). *Robin Hood [1973 animated film]*. Retrieved July 21, 2023 from https://www.imdb.com/title/tt0070608/

IMDb. (2023e,). *Rogues of Sherwood Forest [1959 film]*. Retrieved July 16, 2023 from https://www.imdb.com/title/tt0042901/

Internet Broadway Database. (2001-2024). *Robin Hood - About this show*. Retrieved July 6, 2024 from https://www.ibdb.com/broadway-show/robin-hood-7572

Jonson, B. (1905). *The Sad Shepherd: or, A Tale of Robin Hood*. Retrieved April 26, 2023 from https://d.lib.rochester.edu/robin-hood/text/jonson-sad-shepherd

King Arthur's Knights. (2022). *King Arthur and the Knights of the Round Table*. Retrieved April 22, 2023 from https://kingarthursknights.com/the-knights-of-the-round-table/

King Johnson, K. (2022, 4 January 2022). History of the Opera House: May Valentine, the Robin Hood of opera. *Cheboygan Daily Tribune*. https://www.cheboygannews.com/story/opinion/columns/2022/01/04/history-opera-house-may-valentine-robin-hood-opera/9076625002/

Knight, S. (1994). *Robin Hood: A Complete Study of the English Outlaw*. Wiley–Blackwell.

Knight, S. T. (2000). *Robin Hood and Other Outlaw Tales* (S. Knight & T. Ohlgren, Eds. 2 ed., Vol.). Medieval Institute Publications.

Kroll, J. (2017, 6 March 2017). *Margot Robbie to Star as Maid Marian in 'Robin Hood'-Inspired Film*. Retrieved August 5, 2023 from https://variety.com/2017/film/news/margot-robbie-maid-marian-robin-hood-1202002908/

Lane, E. (2018). *Heart of Sherwood*. Independently Published.

Langland, W. (c.1377). *The Vision of William concerning Piers Plowman in Three Parallel Texts together with Richard the Redeless. Vol I - Text*. Retrieved 19 October, 2023 from https://robinhoodlegend.com/piers-plowman/

Lasky, K. (2010). *Hawksmaid: The Untold Story of Robin Hood and Maid Marian*

Lawhead, S. (2007). *Hood: Book One of The King Raven Trilogy*. Atom

Lawhead, S. R. (2008). *Scarlet: Book Two of The King Ravel Trilogy*. Atom

Lawhead, S. R. (2009). *Tuck: Book Three of The King Ravel Trilogy*. Thomas Nelson Inc; Reprint edition.

Lawton, A. (2018, 25 March 2018). *Rosemary Sutcliff: British writer Rosemary Sutcliff re-makes and re-tells legends of Robin Hood, King Arthur, Beowulf, Tristan and Iseult, Finn Mac Cool and Cuchulain, the Iliad, the Odyssey*. Retrieved June 11, 2023 from https://rosemarysutcliff.com

Liberman, A. (2008, 9 July 2008). *William John Thoms, The Man Who Invented The Word Folklore*. Retrieved April 18, 2023 from https://blog.oup.com/2008/07/folklore/

Longueville, O., & Plummer, J. C. (2018). *Robin Hood's Dawn: Book I The Robin Hood Trilogy* (Vol.). Angevin World Publishing LLC.

Longueville, O., & Plummer, J. C. (2020). *Robin Hood's Widow: Book II The Robin Hood Trilogy*. Angevin World Publishing

Longueville, O., & Plummer, J. C. (2021). *Robin Hood's Return: Book III The Robin Hood Trilogy*. Angevin World Publishing.

Macfarren, G. A. M., & Oxenford, J. L. (1860). Robin Hood - A romantic English Opera in three acts

Performing Edition by Valerie Langfield 2010,. On *Robin Hood* [CD x 2]. Naxos Rights International Ltd. https://www.naxos.com/CatalogueDetail/?id=8.660306-07

Magoon, K. (2016). *Shadows of Sherwood - A Robyn Hoodlum Adventure Book 1*. Bloomsbury Children's USA. https://keklamagoon.com/books/middle-grade/#shadows-of-sherwood

McKinley, R. (1988). *The Outlaws of Sherwood* [ ]. Greenwillow Books. https://en.wikipedia.org/wiki/The_Outlaws_of_Sherwood

McNary, D. (2020, April 10 2020). *'Robin Hood' Animated Film Getting Disney Remake*. Retrieved January 16, 2024 from https://variety.com/2020/film/news/robin-hood-animated-remake-1234577408/

Moke, J. E. M. (2021). *Hood*. Disney Publishing.

Moreland, A. (2021, 7 October 2021). *How we made Robin Hood: the cast and crew of the BBC series look back 15 years later*. Retrieved December 18, 2024 from https://www.radiotimes.com/tv/drama/robin-hood-cast-interview-rt-rewind/

Munday, A. (1601). *Excerpts from The Death of Robert, Earle of Huntington*. Robbins Library Digital Projects. Retrieved October 23, 2023 from https://d.lib.rochester.edu/teams/text/death-of-robert-earle-of-huntington

Munday, A. (2010). *The Downfall of Robert, Earl of Huntingdon. 1601*. Benediction Classics (25 September 2010).

Munday, A., & Chettle, H. (1601). *The Death of Robert, Earle of Huntingdon* Retrieved October23, 2023 from https://reynolds-news.com/2015/06/24/the-downfall-of-robert-earle-of-huntington-1598-the-death-of-robert-earle-of-huntingdon-1601-by-anthony-munday-and-henry-chettle/

Myers, S. (circa 1938, 3 May 2016). *Classic 30s Movie: "The Adventures of Robin Hood"*. Retrieved July 9, 2023 from https://gointothestory.blcklst.com/classic-30s-movie-the-adventures-of-robin-hood-d52ae55d9dcf

Naxos. (2006). *Le Jeu de Robin et de Marion [c. 1282-1283] by Adam de la Halle, recorded by Tonus Peregrinus*. Retrieved November 10, 2024 from https://www.naxos.com/CatalogueDetail/?id=8.557337

Norling, C. A. (2018). *Operatic Egalitarianism: English-language Opera, Redpath Chautauqua, and the May Valentine Opera Company* University of Iowa]. books.google.com.au. https://books.google.com.au/books/about/Operatic_Egalitarianism.html?id=ZdFo0AEACAAJ&redir_esc=y

O'Sullivan, M. (2018, November 20). Who needs another new 'Robin Hood' movie? Absolutely no one. *The Washington Post.* https://www.washingtonpost.com/goingoutguide/movies/who-needs-another-new-robin-hood-movie-absolutely-no-one/2018/11/20/55e21abe-e862-11e8-a939-9469f1166f9d_story.html

Opera Scotland. (n.d.). *Listings and Performance History - Maid Marian by Colin Macleod Campbell and Nancy Campbell.* Retrieved August 6, 2024 from http://operascotland.org/opera/653/Maid+Marian#google_vignette

Parker, M. (2018). *A True Tale of Robin Hood; Setting Forth the Life and Death of That Renowned Out-law [1632].* Gale ECCO, Print Editions (First published in London for T. Cotes, 1632)

Peacock, T. L. (2008). *Maid Marian* (a. D. W. Charles Keller, Ed.). The Gutenberg Project EBook #966. https://www.gutenberg.org/files/966/966-h/966-h.htm#link2HCH0005 (1822)

Peacock, T. L. (2023a). *Maid Marian - Part 1 out of 3 [1822].* Retrieved June 3, 2023 from http://www.fullbooks.com/Maid-Marian1.html

Peacock, T. L. (2023b). *Maid Marian - Part 2 out of 3 [1822].* Retrieved June 3, 2023 from http://www.fullbooks.com/Maid-Marian2.html

Peacock, T. L. (2023c). *Maid Marian - Part 3 out of 3 [1822].* Retrieved June 3, 2023 from http://www.fullbooks.com/Maid-Marian3.html

Peele, G. (2019). *King Edward The First [aka Edward I, 1593].* Retrieved May 9, 2023 from http://elizabethandrama.org/wp-content/uploads/2022/05/Edward-I-Annotated-B.pdf

Perkins, L. F. (1906). *Robin Hood - His Deeds and Adventures as recounted in the old English Ballads; selected and illustrated by Lucy Fitch Perkins. (1906)* [Digitized book]. The Riverside Press, Cambridge, Massachusetts. https://upload.wikimedia.org/wikipedia/commons/3/37/Robin_Hood_-_his_deeds_and_adventures_as_recounted_in_the_old_English_ballads_%28IA_robinhoodhisdeed00per%29.pdf (Boston and New York - Houghton Mifflin Company, The Riverside Press, Cambridge (1923))

Pitcaithly, M. (2013). *Matter of the Greenwood: Maid Marian - Origins.* Retrieved May 9, 2023 from https://www.marcus-pitcaithly.com/single-post/2015/04/18/matter-of-the-greenwood-maid-marian-origins

Pitts, A. (n.d.). *About This Recording - Adam de la Halle (13th century): Le Jeu de Robin et de Marion.* Retrieved May 7, 2023 from https://www.naxos.com/MainSite/Blurbs Reviews/?itemcode=8.557337&catnum=557337&filetype=AboutThisRecording&language=English

Planché, R. J. A., & Bishop, H. R. C. (1822). *Maid Marian; or, Huntress of Arlingford.* John Lowndes, 36, Bow Street, Covent Garden. Retrieved May 03, 2024 from https://d.lib.rochester.edu/robin-hood/text/maid-marian-huntress-of-arlingford

Pyle, H. (2018). *The Merry Adventures of Robin Hood (First Edition): Illustrated Classics*. SeaWolf Press.

Reynolds's News and Miscellany. (2010, 24 June 2015). *The Downfall of Robert, Earle of Huntington (1598) & The Death of Robert, Earle of Huntingdon (1601) by Anthony Munday and Henry Chettle*. Book published by Benediction Classics, Oxford. Retrieved May 24, 2023 from https://reynolds-news.com/2015/06/24/the-downfall-of-robert-earle-of-huntington-1598-the-death-of-robert-earle-of-huntingdon-1601-by-anthony-munday-and-henry-chettle/

Reynolds's News and Miscellany. (2016, 14 October 2016). *Radical Robin Hood: "Little John and Will Scarlet" [1865]*. H. Vickers 1865. Retrieved June 8, 2023 from https://reynolds-news.com/2016/10/14/radical-robin-hood-little-john-and-will-scarlet-1865/

Roberson, J. (1992). *Lady of the Forest: A Novel of Sherwood* (First ed.). Zebra. (1992)

Robinson, S. T. (2023, 3 June 2023). *Maid Marian and her Merry Men [British children's TV series 1989-1994]*. Retrieved July 10, 2023 from https://en.wikipedia.org/w/index.php?title=Maid_Marian_and_Her_Merry_Men&oldid=1158411906

Roehrig, T. (2021). *The Shadows of Sherwood Forest*. Arctis.

Scott, S. W. (2000, 12 April 2023). *Ivanhoe [1820]*. Penguin. https://www.amazon.com.au/Ivanhoe-Sir-Walter-Scott/dp/0140436588

Shea, K. M. (2022a). *Fight for Freedom*. K.M. Shea. https://kmshea.com/book/robyn-hood/

Shea, K. M. (2022b). *Robyn Hood: A Girl's Tale*. K.M. Shea.

Spooner, M. (2019). *Sherwood*. HarperTeen.

Springer, N. (2001, 22 November 22). *Tales of Rowan Hood*. Retrieved July 6, 2023 from https://en.wikipedia.org/w/index.php?title=Tales_of_Rowan_Hood&oldid=1123199915

Stocqueler, J. H. (2010). *Maid Marian, the Forest Queen: A companion to Robin Hood*. The British Library, Historical Print Editions. https://www.amazon.com.au/Marian-Forest-Queen-Being-Companion/dp/B003JH7L6W (1849)

Stover, D. (2013). *Maid Marian and the Lawman*. Bell Bridge Books.

Sutcliff, R. (2013). *The Chronicles of Robin Hood* Red Fox - Mass Market. (1950)

Taylor, D. (2009). *Royal Rebel*. Supernal Friends Publishing. https://www.amazon.com.au/Royal-Rebel-Dana-Taylor-ebook/dp/B0030T1EDK/ref=sr_1_3?crid=2E9ZXSQRBZTKP&keywords=dana+Taylor+Royal+Rebel&qid=1691732826&s=books&sprefix=dana+taylor+royal+rebel%2Cstripbooks%2C291&sr=1-3

Terre Celtiche Blog. (2023). *Child Ballads A-Z: The English and Scottish Popular Ballads*. Retrieved May 7, 2023 from https://terreceltiche.altervista.org/ballad/a-z-list-child-ballads/

The Gilbert and Sullivan Archive. (2017, 13 January 2017). *Maid Marian: Music by Reginald De Koven, Libretto by Harry B. Smith*. Retrieved June 8, 2024 from https://gsarchive.net/AMT/marian/index.html

The Guardian. (2023). *The Adventures of Maid Marian review – historical clunker with a boyband Robin Hood*. Retrieved August 5, 2023 from https://www.theguardian.com/film/2022/may/04/the-adventures-of-maid-marian-review-historical-clunker-with-a-boyband-robin-hood

The Minstrel Henry aka Blind Harry. (2015). *The acts and deeds of the most famous and valiant champion Sir William Wallace, Knight of Ellerslie. Written by Blind Harry in the year 1361. Together with Arnaldi Blair Relationes*. . Gale ECCO, Print Editions.

The Silent Planet Wiki. (n.d.). *Roger Gilbert Lancelyn Green - Biography*. Retrieved May 8, 2023 from https://the-silent-planet.fandom.com/wiki/Roger_Gilbert_Lancelyn_Green

Tomlinson, T. (1995). *The Forestwife. Forestwife Saga. Book 1*. Orchard Books (Orchard Books (1 April 1995))

Tomlinson, T. (1998). *Child of the May. Forestwife Saga. Book 2*. Orchard Books (Orchard Books)

Tomlinson, T. (2000). *The Path of the She Wolf. Forestwife Saga. Book 3*. Red Fox. ( )

Trease, G. (1973). *Bows against the Barons [1934]*. Hodder & Stoughton Ltd; . (1934)

Valdés-Miyares, J. R. (2019, 6 February 2019). *Who was the real Robin Hood?* Retrieved May 16, 2023 from https://www.nationalgeographic.com/history/history-magazine/article/origins-of-england-folk-lore-robin-hood

Vaughn, C. (2020a). *The Ghosts of Sherwood*. Tordotcom.

Vaughn, C. (2020b). *Heirs of Locksley*. Tordotcom.

Victorian Opera Northwest. (2020, 17 September 2020). *Macfarren's Robin Hood (1860)*. Retrieved July 6, 2024 from https://www.victorianoperanorthwest.org/Operas/RobinHood.htm

Vivian, E. C. H. (1965). *The Adventures of Robin Hood [1906]*. Airmont Pub Co. (1906)

Vivian, E. C. H. (1995). *Robin Hood and his Merry Men*. Geddes and Grosset. (1927)

Wallace, S. (2017, 12 August 2017). *Wallace's Wife Marion Braidfute Was Invented?* Retrieved October 20, 2023 from https://clanwallace.org/cw/wallaces-wife-marion-braidfute-was-invented/

Watson, E. (2004). *Maid Marian*. Three Rivers Press.

White, T. H. (1962). *The Once And Future King*. Fontana/Collins. https://en.wikipedia.org/wiki/The_Once_and_Future_King

Bibliography

Wikipedia. (2021, 25 October 2021). *Maud le Vavasour, Baroness Butler.* Retrieved May 13, 2023 from https://en.wikipedia.org/w/index.php?title=Maud_le_Vavasour,_Baroness_Butler&oldid=1051743338#

Wikipedia. (2022, 28 July 2022). *The Foresters [Play by Alfred, Lord Tennyson].* Retrieved June 8, 2023 from https://en.wikipedia.org/w/index.php?title=The_Foresters&oldid=1101032853

Wikipedia. (2023a, 31 March 2023). *Adam de la Halle [French poet/composer].* Retrieved May 7, 2023 from https://en.wikipedia.org/w/index.php?title=Adam_de_la_Halle&oldid=1147446754

Wikipedia. (2023b). *The Adventures of Robin Hood [1938 film].* Retrieved April 17, 2023 from https://en.wikipedia.org/w/index.php?title=The_Adventures_of_Robin_Hood&oldid=1150710292

Wikipedia. (2023c, 20 June 2023). *The adventures of Robin Hood [tv series, 1955-1959].* Retrieved July 10, 2023 from https://en.wikipedia.org/w/index.php?title=The_Adventures_of_Robin_Hood_(TV_series)&oldid=1161016793

Wikipedia. (2023d, 8 March 2023). *A Challenge for Robin Hood [1967 film].* Retrieved June 26, 2023 from https://en.wikipedia.org/w/index.php?title=A_Challenge_for_Robin_Hood&oldid=1143606551

Wikipedia. (2023e, 5 March 2023). *Douglas Fairbanks in Robin Hood [1922 film].* Retrieved April 17, 2023 from https://en.wikipedia.org/w/index.php?title=Douglas_Fairbanks_in_Robin_Hood&oldid=1142949918

Wikipedia. (2023f, 13 May 2023). *A Gest of Robyn Hode, aka A Lyttell Geste of Robyn Hode [circa 1493-1518].* Retrieved May 13, 2023 from https://en.wikipedia.org/w/index.php?title=A_Gest_of_Robyn_Hode&oldid=1154549156

Wikipedia. (2023g, 12 February 2023). *Joachim Hayward Stocqueler [1801-1886].* Retrieved June 2, 2023 from https://en.wikipedia.org/w/index.php?title=Joachim_Hayward_Stocqueler&oldid=1138975910

Wikipedia. (2023h, 5 April 2023). *Johann Gottfried Herder [1744-1803].* Retrieved April 18, 2023 from https://en.wikipedia.org/w/index.php?title=Johann_Gottfried_Herder&oldid=1148365264

Wikipedia. (2023i, 14 May 2023). *Lady of Sherwood [1999 book by Jennifer Roberson].* Retrieved June 29, 2023 from https://en.wikipedia.org/w/index.php?title=Lady_of_Sherwood&oldid=1154679378

Wikipedia. (2023j, 28 May 2023). *Lady of the Forest.* https://en.wikipedia.org/wiki/Lady_of_the_Forest#:~:text=In%20an%20article%20published%20in,as%20isolated%20difficulties%22%20-%20Marian%20for

Wikipedia. (2023k, 18 October 2023). *Morris dance.* Retrieved October 19, 2023 from https://en.wikipedia.org/w/index.php?title=Morris_dance&oldid=1180753672

Wikipedia. (2023l, 8 April 2023). *The New Adventures of Robin Hood [TV series 1997]*. Retrieved August 5, 2023 from https://en.wikipedia.org/w/index.php?title=The_New_Adventures_of_Robin_Hood&oldid=1148845560

Wikipedia. (2023m, 1 August 2023). *Once Upon a Time [TV series 2011-2018]*. Retrieved August 6, 2023 from https://en.wikipedia.org/w/index.php?title=Once_Upon_a_Time_(TV_series)&oldid=1168167107

Wikipedia. (2023n, 27 January 2023). *Penny Dreadful*. Retrieved June 9, 2023 from https://en.wikipedia.org/w/index.php?title=Penny_dreadful&oldid=1135926198

Wikipedia. (2023o, 15 May 2023). *Pierce Egan the Younger [1814-1880]*. Retrieved June 2, 2023 from https://en.wikipedia.org/w/index.php?title=Pierce_Egan_the_Younger&oldid=1154875272

Wikipedia. (2023p, 27 May 2023). *Princess of Thieves [2001 TV movie]*. Retrieved July 21, 2023 from https://en.wikipedia.org/w/index.php?title=Princess_of_Thieves&oldid=1157285066

Wikipedia. (2023q, 12 April 2023). *Robert Fitzwalter*. Retrieved May 13, 2023 from https://en.wikipedia.org/w/index.php?title=Robert_Fitzwalter&oldid=1149431075

Wikipedia. (2023r, 9 May 2023). *Robin and Marian [1976 film]*. Retrieved June 7, 2023 from https://en.wikipedia.org/w/index.php?title=Robin_and_Marian&oldid=1153998982

Wikipedia. (2023s, 26 June 2023). *Robin and the 7 Hoods [1964 film]*. Retrieved June 29, 2023 from https://en.wikipedia.org/w/index.php?title=Robin_and_the_7_Hoods&oldid=1161996558

Wikipedia. (2023t, 01 August 2023). *Robin Hood (De Koven opera)*. Retrieved May 16, 2024 from https://en.wikipedia.org/wiki/Robin_Hood_(De_Koven_opera)

Wikipedia. (2023u, 18 January 2023). *Robin Hood [1953 TV series]*. Retrieved July 10, 2023 from https://en.wikipedia.org/w/index.php?title=Robin_Hood_(1953_TV_series)&oldid=1134465023

Wikipedia. (2023v, 20 June 2023). *Robin Hood [1973 animated film]*. Retrieved June 26, 2023 from https://en.wikipedia.org/wiki/Robin_Hood_(1973_film)#:~:text=Robin%20Hood%20is%20a%201973,21st%20Disney%20animated%20feature%20film.

Wikipedia. (2023w, 26 January 2023). *Robin Hood [1990 TV series]*. Retrieved August 6, 2023 from https://en.wikipedia.org/w/index.php?title=Robin_Hood_(1990_TV_series)&oldid=1135803409

Wikipedia. (2023x, 10 January 2023). *Robin Hood [1991 British film]*. Retrieved June 25, 2023 from https://en.wikipedia.org/w/index.php?title=Robin_Hood_(1991_British_film)&oldid=1132779384

Wikipedia. (2023y, 26 April 2023). *Robin Hood [2006 TV series]*. Retrieved August 6, 2023 from https://en.wikipedia.org/w/index.php?title=Robin_Hood_(2006_TV_series)&oldid=1151813482

Wikipedia. (2023z, 22 July 2023). *Robin Hood [2010 film]*. Retrieved July 23, 2023 from https://en.wikipedia.org/w/index.php?title=Robin_Hood_(2010_film)&oldid=1166533852

Wikipedia. (2023aa, 17 June 2023). *Robin Hood [2018 film]*. Retrieved July 23, 2023 from https://en.wikipedia.org/w/index.php?title=Robin_Hood_(2018_film)&oldid=1160609637

Wikipedia. (2023ab, 26 April 2023). *Robin Hood [Heroic Outlaw]*. Retrieved May 15, 2023 from https://en.wikipedia.org/w/index.php?title=Robin_Hood&oldid=1151835653

Wikipedia. (2023ac, 19 July 2023). *Robin Hood: Mischief in Sherwood [TV animated series 2015-2019]*. Retrieved August 7, 2023 from https://en.wikipedia.org/w/index.php?title=Robin_Hood:_Mischief_in_Sherwood&oldid=1166178600

Wikipedia. (2023ad). *Robin Hood: Prince of Thieves [1991 film]*. Retrieved April 17, 2023 from https://en.m.wikipedia.org/w/index.php?title=Robin_Hood:_Prince_of_Thieves&oldid=1149484017

Wikipedia. (2023ae, 29 June 2023). *Robin of Sherwood - TV series [1984-1986]*. Retrieved July 10, 2023 from https://en.wikipedia.org/w/index.php?title=Robin_of_Sherwood&oldid=1162499144

Wikipedia. (2023af, 23 January 2023). *Robot of Sherwood - episode 3 of series 8: Doctor Who [BBC TV series 2014]*. Retrieved August 6, 2023 from https://en.wikipedia.org/w/index.php?title=Robot_of_Sherwood&oldid=1135261061

Wikipedia. (2023ag, 2 July 2023). *Rocket Robin Hood [animated TV series 1966-1969]*. Retrieved August 6, 2023 from https://en.wikipedia.org/w/index.php?title=Rocket_Robin_Hood&oldid=1163013692

Wikipedia. (2023ah, 20 June 2023). *Rogues of Sherwood Forest [1959 film]*. Retrieved July 16, 2023 from https://en.wikipedia.org/w/index.php?title=Rogues_of_Sherwood_Forest&oldid=1161013127

Wikipedia. (2023ai, 23 April 2023). *The story of Robin Hood [1952 film]*. Retrieved July 18, 2023 from https://en.wikipedia.org/w/index.php?title=The_Story_of_Robin_Hood_(film)&oldid=1151377403

Wikipedia. (2023aj, 8 March 2023). *Sword of Sherwood Forest [1960 film]*. Retrieved June 29, 2023 from https://en.wikipedia.org/w/index.php?title=Sword_of_Sherwood_Forest&oldid=1143606251

Wikipedia. (2023ak, 26 May 2023). *Thomas Love Peacock [1785-1866]*. Retrieved June 1, 2023 from https://en.wikipedia.org/w/index.php?title=Thomas_Love_Peacock&oldid=1157170741

Wikipedia. (2023al, 29 July 2023). *Young Robin Hood [animated tv series 1991-1992]*. Retrieved August 6, 2023 from https://en.wikipedia.org/w/index.php?title=Young_Robin_Hood&oldid=1167757410

Wikipedia. (2024a, 27 June 2024). *Chautauqua*. Retrieved July 4, 2024 from https://en.wikipedia.org/wiki/Chautauqua

Wikipedia. (2024b, 19 June 2024). *The Faerie Queene by Edmund Spenser. 1590-1596.*. Retrieved June 25, 2024 from https://en.wikipedia.org/wiki/The_Faerie_Queene

Wikipedia. (2024c, 12 September 2024). *Merry Men*. Retrieved November 4, 2024 from https://en.wikipedia.org/wiki/Merry_Men

Wikipedia. (2024d, 26 December 2024). *Wolfshead: The Legend of Robin Hood*. https://en.wikipedia.org/wiki/Wolfshead:_The_Legend_of_Robin_Hood

Wiseman, A. (2024, 03 May 2024). *Hugh Jackman & Jodie Comer To Star In Robin Hood Reimagining 'The Death Of Robin Hood' For 'A Quiet Place: Day One' Director Michael Sarnoski — Cannes Market Hot Project*. Retrieved May 4, 2024 from https://deadline.com/2024/05/hugh-jackman-jodie-comer-death-robin-hood-michael-sarnoski-cannes-market-1235903543/?fbclid=PAZXh0bgNhZW0CMTEAAaZXr6RXKSbNpSujx7hMd6jIMA4tzK0hzDKVyVqrb3gOq30-PdlMEZ84Uv8_aem_AXIUJTecbjFPs0D4Qd1VVt1EufU0PsJC3ewV2ANpee5DOv4Hy_RGYQMQji-EslXE38k2xbVr3r7MtbtGDQ2-yRXL

Wright, A. W. (2022, October 2022). *Robin Hood Spotlight: Douglas Fairbanks in Robin Hood 1922 Silent Film*. Retrieved July 16, 2023 from https://www.boldoutlaw.com/robspot/douglas-fairbanks-in-robin-hood.html

About The Author

Lydia-Jane Plante has had a lifelong interest in books and writing. She has a Master of Social Science degree which fostered an ongoing interest in the social and cultural aspects of human behavior. She also has an enduring interest in British Social History. Lydia-Jane lives in Australia, on Queensland's Sunshine Coast, where she enjoys a relaxed lifestyle which enables her to pursue her love of writing.